In the Presence of
High Beings

To My Friends
with Much Love

Mark

: PREPAIR To BE AMAZED ! :

IN THE PRESENCE OF

high beings

WHAT DOLPHINS WANT YOU TO KNOW

BOBBIE SANDOZ-MERRILL, MSW

COUNCIL OAK BOOKS
SAN FRANCISCO / TULSA

Council Oak Books, Tulsa OK 74104
www.counciloakbooks.com

© 1999, 2005 by Bobbie Sandoz-Merrill

Cover Design by Buffy Terry
Interior Design by Vanessa Perez

Library of Congress Cataloging-in-Publication Data

Sandoz-Merrill, Bobbie.
 In the presence of high beings : what dolphins want you to know / Bobbie Sandoz-Merrill.
     p. cm.
 Rev. ed. of: Listening to wild dolphins. c1999.
 Includes bibliographical references.
 ISBN 1-57178-179-X
1. Self-actualization (Psychology) 2. Dolphins--Psychology. 3. Dolphins--Therapeutic use. 4. Human-animal communication--Case studies. I. Sandoz-Merrill, Bobbie. Listening to wild dolphins. II. Title.
 BF637.S4S26 2005

                          2004025645

With gratitude to the dolphins for their kind friendship, joyful wisdom, and loving patience with our slowness to listen to the language of other species and better worlds.

contents

**PART 3: CREATING THE WORLD OF YOUR DREAMS:
SIX INSIGHTS FOR MANIFESTING GOALS**

PART 4: THE FUTURE

acknowledgments

i am grateful first to my husband, Dr. Tom Merrill, for inspiring in me a desire to live my life fully and to its completion with all the richness, joy, and possibilities I am capable of reaching. With his help, I have learned to dance with my human partner in ways even more blissful than my dances with the dolphins. This is one of the most important things they came to teach me . . . and the mission is complete.

I am grateful to Council Oak Books for seeing the value of my dolphin book and for publishing this expanded and completed version of their story and lessons.

I am particularly grateful to Publisher Paulette Millichap for so graciously hosting our first meeting in Chicago, her openness to the possibilities in life, and for making things happen.

I am also grateful to Paulette's daughter, Kelly Hauf, for meeting with me in Hawaii and letting me know before I met with the others that I was in good hands with good people.

And I am deeply grateful to the Associate Publisher of Council Oak Books, Ja-lene Clark, for her delightful mixture of easy friendship and polished professionalism. She too sees the gems in life and has a gift in polishing them to their full brilliance.

I am grateful to Buffy Terry, the designer of the cover, and for the inspiration it provided me while finishing the book.

I am also grateful to Sally Dennison, Senior Editor, for her beautiful work, easy nature, good ideas, and for helping me with my computer.

And, I am grateful to Laura Wood, Charlotte Stewart, Rick Hauf, Jennifer Beard, Irene Dennis, and Bert Reaves for all the things they have done to bring this book to completion and get it into the bookstores.

I am also grateful to my readers for their interest in the dolphins and whales, their caring about how we treat them and each other, and for learning their startling lessons about reaching higher and becoming a greater humanity.

And I am grateful to my children, grandchildren, stepchildren, and step-grandchildren for their varying roles in my dolphin journey and for inspiring me to keep my eye on living the kind of life that will protect their futures.

And, finally, I am grateful to God for the experience of swimming with the dolphins and for so elegantly bringing sheer magic and pure grace to my life.

introduction

when I first began fifteen years ago to swim with dolphins and whales in the wild, life for me was markedly different. Life for people in the United States was also different, as was life for the dolphins and whales.

I was nearing the end of a long marriage and was on the threshold of many changes and an uncertain future. And so I used this time to apply the messages I had learned from the dolphins about how to become my best self and manifest my dreams. I worked diligently with their messages every morning before starting my day, and within a year of publishing the book, I had manifested everything on my list, including finding a relationship I thought might be "the one."

But then an odd thing happened. A year earlier, I had placed the name of only one specific man on my list of possibilities. Although we had met in childhood and had even enjoyed a daylong crush on each other, I would not have considered him as a potential partner if it had not been for one conversation we had enjoyed as adults.

Yet as soon as I put his name on my list, during a meditation that followed, I felt a "click" within myself that caused me to feel strongly that we would reconnect and finish our lives as partners. Time passed, nothing happened, and I soon forgot about this and began dating others. Close to a year later, right after making a call to arrange taking a condo in another city for a few months to finish writing a book and also to explore the possibilities of the relationship I thought was "the one," I bumped into this man from my youth.

We fell instantly in love, and no exploring was necessary. Now, four years later we are still joyfully married and grateful for our "chance" meeting that day. But the important part of this story is that as a result of our both being and behaving as our higher selves in the relationship—in much the way the dolphins behave—we are even more in love today. In fact, we recently launched our first co-authored book, *Settle for More,* about how to stay in love with the partners who capture our hearts and enjoy a lasting and growing partnership. My life is now replete with a sense of renewal, and we are in the midst of a wonderful journey together, filled with all manner of possibilities.

But things have not gone as well for United States citizens in general. It seems that following 9/11, as a result of focusing so much of our energy on our fears and resisting the things we don't like in lieu of attending to our possibilities, we have experienced deep losses in many arenas. In fact, I am reminded of the story I read as a child of the woman with holes in her blanket who decided to solve her problem by cutting out the holes. I feel our approach to the 9/11 problem has been equally narrow in vision and often wonder how long our "blanket" will last.

Things have not been completely pleasant for the dolphins and whales during this period, either, although in contrast to the struggles in which people are engaged throughout the landscape above the sea, they have managed in the midst of their crisis to remain "high beings." Although I shared in my introduction to the first edition of this book that the dolphins had increased their interest in befriending humans about fifteen years before and were meeting with more and more of us to play along the shorelines of our world, a dramatic event seems to have caused them to retreat. When our country slipped lethal sonar past environmental laws into the oceans that serve as their home, we caused massive worldwide strandings of our cetacean friends. Their withdrawal from so much friendliness and play was immediately apparent, prompting painful reflection on who we are when we act in this dishonorable way.

However, after a few years of reducing their levels of play with us, the dolphins and whales have now found a way to help us move to a higher plane of awareness and behavior, all the while remaining loving in the process. They also demonstrated their remarkable level of consciousness in the way in which they orchestrated this, although many humans persist in denying this aspect of these wonderful beings or their role in exposing the sonar problem, as discussed in the final chapter of this book.

In this edition, the original message is the same, offering us a clear model of our potential and clear steps for reaching it. Yet here, there is also a new, even more important message for us. And if we learn all the dolphins have to tell us—including the message introduced in this revised edition—we will not only recover our losses, but can have the lives we always wanted. In short, *In the Presence of High Beings* shows us not only how to be our best selves and realize our greatest desires, but also how to achieve this even after making colossal errors and cutting away most of the blanket beneath which we hide in our clumsy efforts to correct them.

The additional message from the dolphins delivered here offers us the only chance we have: a way to use the miraculous power of love to solve the kinds of problems we have created above and below the sea. The message is wrapped into a shocking story about the lethal sonar in our oceans and how the dolphins remain high-level beings in the face of our killing their species.

Filled with intrigue, this story offers us final proof of the level of evolution the dolphins and whales have reached. It also shows us how they, like other truly high beings, do not lower lower themselves in order to battle the many low places we humans have assumed, but wait patiently while calling us to join them at the top. They are also clear that the choice is ours. And even if we destroy them before we make that higher choice, they will remain true to who they are. If we do not make it, neither will they. Meanwhile, they offer us the amazing opportunity to be *In the Presence of High Beings*.

With aloha and blessings,
Bobbie Sandoz-Merrill

guidelines for successful cetacean encounters

my personal favorite guides for seeing the dolphins in the bay described in this book are: Tori and Armin Cullins, 808.306.7273, http://sailhawaii.com WildSide@SailHawaii.com

Wild Side Specialty Tours. Non-profit portion of proceeds go to Wild Dolphin Foundation

The following guidelines are for both swimmers and boaters wishing to observe or swim with dolphins as well as whales in those countries where it is allowed.

To have a successful encounter with dolphins and whales, either from the water in places where it is legal or from boats, it's critical to follow a number of guidelines. In fact, without these guidelines, attempts to make a connection may prove dangerous to the dolphins and whales and/or the swimmers and boaters.

To begin, the most important component for a successful cetacean encounter is to approach dolphins and whales with the same care you would afford a respected being from your own species. Be aware that only dolphin- and whale-initiated encounters constitute swimming with these wonderful beings. Chasing after them is simply not the same experience and in fact prevents you from having one. In addition, jet skis should never be used for this purpose, as the level of their noise acoustically confuses cetaceans and proves dangerous to them, as well as the jet skiers and other swimmers in the area.

- Boaters and swimmers should never chase, block, crowd, or box cetaceans, nor should they approach them from the front or back or from a perpendicular angle, while moving directly at them.

- Approach should always be made slowly and with care, only from the side, in a parallel manner, leaving one hundred yards of space for large boats, at least two full boat lengths for smaller boats, and about fifteen to twenty feet for swimmers.

- Anytime dolphins or whales change course to move away from you, even if you are approaching correctly, never pursue them.

- If the dolphins and whales then wish to get closer, they will slowly move toward the swimmer or boater, while the swimmer or boater remains stationery or continues to swim in a parallel manner along with the cetacean. This prevents any confusion about the distance the cetacean would like to create between the swimmer or boater and cetacean, clearly allowing them to choose and establish the desired distance.

- Always leave plenty of space for dolphins or whales to approach you on their own time and at their own pace. By doing this, you not only show respect for the cetaceans but create the kinds of conditions that could lead to a very successful encounter.

- No more than two boats should approach cetaceans at any given time, and the second boat should remain behind the first one. In Australia and Mexico, where I have witnessed the best encounters, boatsmen are highly respectful of each other and take turns rather than crowd each other out. As a result, the cetaceans remain considerably longer—often for one to several hours—and they tend to visit each of the boats involved during the time they interact with the humans.

- The same type of approach is true for swimmers. No more than two to four should approach cetaceans at any given time, and the second swimmer should either be holding the hand of the first swimmer or remain behind the first one there. The third swimmer should remain behind the second, and the fourth behind the third. When people are cooperative in this manner and remain friendly with each other, the dolphins and whales enjoy the positive energy among them and are more likely to stay with the group and approach, whereas when people become competitive, the cetaceans invariably leave.

- When this approach is followed, dolphins and whales feel free to remain in the area and usually visit everyone there. By contrast, when boats and swimmers crowd around a dolphin or whale, they invariably dive or leave the area, usually immediately.

- Engine noises should be as quiet as possible, since cetaceans are acoustically sensitive. If dolphins or whales approach your boat, slow down, then stop, and put your engine into idle. This reduces the sound but gives them an auditory fix on your position. The exception to this is when dolphins seem to be interested in bow-riding. If this is the case, watch very carefully and allow them to ride while maintaining your speed or slowing down...without going so slowly that they lose interest. Be aware however, that sometimes a slower pace will cause mothers to allow their babies to bow ride, either with the mothers accompanying them or on their own.

- Once cetaceans are around your boat, it is important that you remain there until they leave, since changes in your movement could confuse their auditory senses and cause a collision. Consequently they must be at least twenty-five yards away before it is safe to very slowly and carefully move away.

- If swimmers enter the water from a boat, it is best to do so very quietly, again approaching the cetaceans from the side at a parallel angle rather than meeting them head-on or chasing them from behind. Swimmers should leave about fifteen to twenty feet between themselves and the dolphins to allow the dolphins to approach them only if desired.

- When there are swimmers in the water, other boats must remain a hundred yards away from the activity.

- It's important not to reach for dolphins or whales or attempt to grab their dorsals or tails in an effort to ride them. This is almost never a part of a wild cetacean / human interaction, especially with a pod or group of dolphins. If touch is to be a part of your experience, it is critical that the dolphin is the one to initiate it. Those who reach out will learn the hard way that this will invariably abort their encounter.

- Leave all jewelry and other manufactured toys and objects at home since these can injure the dolphins and attract barracuda.

- Similarly, an injured or bleeding swimmer (menses included) should avoid open ocean swimming due to the possibility of attracting predators such as sharks.

- Begin your swim with quiet, calm motions and allow the dolphin or whale to take the lead rather than try to set the pace yourself.

- Never feed dolphins or whales. This causes a serious disruption to their social order. It also changes the way these otherwise peaceful beings approach humans and can stimulate aggression, biting, and pulling people underwater. In fact, reports of "dangerous" interactions with dolphins and whales, when traced, seem to be connected to the dolphins and whales having been fed by humans in the past or during the identified dangerous encounter.

- Be sensitive to the needs of the dolphins and whales. If they are in a state of rest, swimming meditatively, breathing together as a group, involved in a funeral, or are otherwise not showing an interest in you, do not approach them.

- If dolphins swim directly at you nodding their heads aggressively, slapping their tails, or clapping their jaws, these are indications of boundary setting, and you should drop out immediately.

- On the other hand, if they are looking at you, rolling over, waving a pectoral tail or fin at you, or acting as if they want to connect, it is OK to make yourself available for an interaction in accordance with the guidelines. You will be most successful if you become passive and let them approach you. If you swim toward them instead, you risk provoking their immediate departure. You may see them swim under you as they leave, but by being impatient and swimming toward them in this way, you have interrupted the next level of your interaction.

- Avoid sudden, noisy, or unexpected changes in your behavior, as this may startle the dolphins or whales.

- Although dolphins and whales like music and drumming and will often approach if they hear it, new, sudden sounds occurring while they are approaching or after they first arrive will tend to scare them off.

- It is important that everyone accept responsibility for behaving maturely, rather than break the rules of common courtesy and stimulate governmental restrictions to be imposed on these special interspecies interactions.

- Whenever dolphins decide to swim with you, they will slowly move toward you or under you. They usually start anywhere from twenty to thirty feet away from you but may then slowly move closer, getting as near as fifteen feet from you for your first swim. As they get to know you better, they may draw even closer, sometimes as close as one or two feet from you. But this only happens if you give them the time to initiate this level of closeness and you refrain from reaching out to touch them.

- Give the dolphins and whales the gift of your loving heart, music, joy, and bow-riding.

- Arrive as guests, not hosts, and students, not teachers.

- Take great pleasure in the gift of whatever friendship the dolphins and whales offer you, and open your heart to the full extent of gratitude the experience evokes within you. Enjoy!

a magical garden
beneath the sea

CHAPTER 1

dolphin connections

Stay as aware of your thoughts and behaviors as you would if a respected master were watching, since this will prompt your higher self to come forth in an effort to impress him.

I had spent most of my adult years as a therapist, partnering with my clientele in their pursuit of goals, from clearing away blocks to fulfilling their highest potential and attaining greater joy. Like me, most of them appeared to be generally successful people who simply wanted more. In fact, it was always a mystery to me that there were so many of us in this category who would be envied by others, while in the privacy of our own self-awareness we felt something was missing. Thus, as I worked to help my clients uncover the secret to increasing happiness, I too pursued deeper levels of clarity and joy.

Having reared two children, written a book on parenting, worked as a columnist for my local newspaper, and kept to an active schedule of public speaking, I had discovered a number of roads to the happiness we sought together. Yet after all these years, some significant pieces still eluded us.

Ten years ago, when this story first begins, I was caught in a particularly uncertain period in my life. My kids, who had brought so much aliveness and joy to our family, had recently graduated from college and made their final moves out of our home. In response to this ending, I began a new and challenging venture, preparing for partial retirement and full-time authorship by reducing the counseling practice I had developed for more than twenty years. But one evening as I sat on the rocks watching the dolphins glide through the Kahala Mandarin Hotel's languid lagoon, what really held my attention was the turmoil in my marriage.

As I looked into the pool for solace, little did I suspect that what was about to happen would open an unforeseen door that would lead to new levels of bliss and joy. Neither did I know that I was about to find the key I had been seeking to my next level of happiness—a universal key, no less, that would work for anyone, no matter what state of contentment they enjoyed or what levels they had reached in their personal journeys.

I had quietly separated from my first husband a few years before, yet we continued to live as roommates in a house we couldn't sell and had managed in the process to rekindle our friendship. In fact, we had recently reconciled enough to give our union one more try. Yet the moment we thought our marriage might still work, the fighting resumed.

We had just had another spat when my husband abandoned our beach walk to go wait in the car. I was sitting on the lagoon rocks watching the dolphins I had befriended at the start of our separation, puzzling over what to do next. Then in my early fifties, I had committed most of my adult years to this marriage, and the thought of finishing life's journey alone following such a big investment stirred anxious feelings in me.

As I was thus uneasily musing, Maka, one of the hotel's dolphins, swam up to me toting a tourist's visor under his fin. He then let it go, dove clumsily under the water, and surfaced with the hat askew on his head as his gaze danced playfully into mine. When I burst out laughing, Maka seemed pleased. He repeated his antics until my mood shifted and I was left chuckling beside the lagoon.

The hotel dolphins always had a joyful effect on me, and I had grown to love them deeply over the past few years. In fact, my bond with them had relieved some of the loneliness of my separation, as

I knew they were available and willing to lift my spirits and restore peace to my heart during these moments of connection. I wasn't sure what it was about the dolphins that moved me so much, but I knew they had a wonderful effect on my emotions.

Iwa (pronounced Eva), the closest of my dolphin friends, approached after Maka had completed his mission. She positioned herself upright in the water before me and locked her gaze into mine. I had never seen her sit upright in front of anyone before, nor had she ever looked at me in this direct manner. Her eyes were usually very penetrating, but now they seemed to look past me to something beyond.

As I puzzled over what she was seeing, I felt a charge of energy shoot briefly through me, which left as quickly as it had come. I felt mysteriously honored by the upright position Iwa continued to hold as she fixed her soulful gaze on me—yet I remained perplexed by its meaning. Whatever it was, it had caused a surge of soothing tears to well up within me, and my fear of being alone seemed to wash away. It was as though she had recharged the energies of my heart.

This was the first time I had felt so valued by Maka and Iwa in one sitting, and although they usually acknowledged or played with me in some manner, they were also capable of ignoring me in favor of other visitors. Or, one might give me his or her attention while the other watched furtively from a distance but refused to make contact. Thus, I felt especially blessed that this evening had proffered a special visit from each of them.

My favorite dolphin had been moved to another location, and I still grieved her loss. Nehoa was an older "auntie" (a Hawaiian term for "close friend") and the first of the lagoon dolphins to adopt the pattern of carrying hats under her fins, an activity she began soon after Iwa's son Hoku was born.

Although Nehoa had tried in the beginning to help care for the newborn calf, as females in the wild are known to do, it was clear that Iwa preferred to tend to Hoku by herself. Then one day, perhaps giving up on the idea of helping Iwa, Nehoa fetched a tourist's hat that had blown into the lagoon and tucked it under her fin. It seemed as though she had found a baby of her own to tend and was proud of her new acquisition.

It didn't take long for Nehoa to gain a good deal of attention for carrying her hat, and she began to swim with a pronounced strut along the edge of the lagoon displaying it with pride, sometimes even rolling over on her side to show it off better. It was clear that Nehoa was getting as much recognition for her hat as Iwa and her baby received, and she particularly enjoyed posing with it for photographs. Before long, carrying the prized hat became Nehoa's trademark, and she was soon viewed as a special part of the hotel's dolphin experience.

Over time, people began to toss additional hats to Nehoa, which she also enjoyed carrying, one under each fin, as she showed them off alternately. Because red was her favorite color, she usually had a red hat or two tucked away and was particularly reluctant to surrender these to her trainer at the end of the day. Nehoa appreciated the kick I got out of her hats and always swam up to me the moment I arrived to show me her latest acquisition.

Sadly, the day came when it was decided that young Hoku needed to be moved from the lagoon to another site to be separated from his dominant father, Maka, and "Auntie" Nehoa was selected to accompany him. This move would also separate her from the increasingly temperamental Maka, who had developed a pattern common to dominant males in captivity of picking on females as well.

Only Hoku's mother, Iwa, was left behind with Maka at the luxurious hotel site, since she was better able to manage his more temperamental nature. My heart went out to Nehoa, for I knew that she would live out her life in the smaller facility further from my home, and that I would miss regular connections with this sweet dolphin.

It was only after Nehoa's departure that Iwa and I became more connected. Our friendship began when I first noticed that she often swam up to me soon after my arrival at the hotel. She would then glide back and forth in front of me with an unblinking eye fixed on mine, as I gazed with equal intensity back at her. I often felt locked into these gazes, lost in a dreamy and delightful trance, as Iwa pulled me through the portals of her eyes to rest in her heart. Next she would turn and aim the top of her head toward me in a deliberate manner and then turn back to look at me again. We would resume our gaze and remain connected for extended periods. I soon learned to pull her into my heart as well. During these meetings of the heart, we would bathe each other in love, and I always came away feeling as though I was emerging from deep meditation.

To return to the evening of the spat with my huband, I felt lighter and more serene after sitting on the rocks and connecting with my two dolphin friends. Thus, I returned with renewed peace to the car and my waiting husband, who apologized for his irritability, which made forgiving him far easier for me.

A short time later I met a man who had been swimming with dolphins for about a year in the open ocean. He reported that, although dolphins are rarely mentioned in early Hawaiian lore, increasingly dolphins were befriending swimmers in Hawaiian waters, much like the whales in Mexico who approach people on boats and get close enough to be touched. These whale encounters had come to be known as "the friendly whale phenomenon," and the whales who engaged in them were recognized by the Mexican locals as "las amistosas," or "the friendlies."

I had heard about these meetings with amiable dolphins and whales who swim free in the ocean, and I yearned to connect with them myself. Thus, I embarked on a search for the friendly Hawaiian dolphins with a group of friends I had grown up with in our beloved Hawaii. Although my friends and I had a good deal of fun and drew closer on these outings, we didn't encounter dolphins during this initial quest, though we once heard their chirps and knew they were nearby.

Meanwhile, my husband's curiosity about the dolphins was growing, and he decided one day to join me in this venture. We planned to drive the following morning to a bay so beautifully marbled with turquoise and blue that Hawaiian royalty had chosen its cove and the velvet valley overlooking it for their summer playground. Now a pod of friendly dolphins frolicked in its beauty and were known to periodically connect with swimmers who came to its shores.

Unfortunately, as my husband and I set out the next morning, we got into yet another of our spats, which lasted for the duration of our drive. Although dolphins were reported to have been playing in the bay prior to our arrival, they left before we got there. This happened again a few weeks later, and we began to suspect that our quarreling might be unattractive to these good-natured beings.

Our hunch was confirmed by people familiar with the dolphins, who reported that they approach some swimmers right away but make others wait. It seemed they intended to enable the rebuffed people to become more aware of what in them might be unattractive and require healing. In my own case, as I began to reflect on what in me might need correction, it didn't take long to uncover the problem. My energies and my husband's had become increasingly quarrelsome because we had each looked to the other to change rather than address what in ourselves needed healing. With this in mind, we sat together in a kayak in the bay on our third day, each letting go of our anger and blame, as well listening more attentively and accepting more responsibility for our respective parts in the problems between us. Our communication that day was better than it had been in thirty years of marriage, and we felt more peaceful as we sat in the kayak, fulfilled by what had transpired.

When we returned to shore, others on the beach reported that the dolphins had been circling in a wide swath around us. Although we never saw them, we had felt their calming presence throughout our talk, and the day marked the beginning of a more healing relationship. After this experience we knew that, whether or not we stayed together, we would always treat one another with greater caring and respect.

a prelude to lessons

Further into my experience with the dolphins, it became apparent that they were presenting me with a series of lessons about how humans can act as their higher selves and manifest the world of their dreams. But it was only after this became clear that I was able to look back and realize that they had given me a very important key to my happiness that day on the bay. The insight was this: *In order to draw the goodness of life to you, you must be attractive to your dreams.* This lesson was so simple I had almost missed it. Yet the truth of this idea is particularly significant in view of new developments from progressive scientists such as Candace Pert *(Molecules of Emotion,* 1997), revealing how we attract various things to us, even at the molecular level, in accordance with the energies that we actively hold within us. This explains why anytime we feel insecure or angry, we repel our positive desires, whereas, when we are filled with confidence and joy, we attract good things.

Accordingly, the next time my husband and I drove to the bay, we did so in peace, and the dolphins rewarded our newly attained attractiveness with the gift of our first connection with them.

anytime you are filled with
attractive energies,
the goodness of life will draw near
and shower its blessings on you.

CHAPTER 2

first encounters

Immerse yourself in the joy of each moment rather than submit to the repelling energies of disappointment simply because future dreams have not yet arrived.

As we parked our car at the edge of the bay, a single dolphin leaped teasingly out of the water just a few feet from shore and glanced briefly in our direction before returning to the sea. We had never seen a dolphin that close to the beach, and we sensed that he had come to herald a day of swimming with the dolphins.

My breath quickened as I felt this call to play, and my husband and I scurried about excitedly to gather our things together. By the time we made our way down the path to the beach, a handful of swimmers was emerging from the water. They had enjoyed a fulfilling encounter with the dolphins and were ready for a rest. My heart sank with worry that we had come too late, although I tried to remain calm as we grabbed our snorkeling gear and ran to the water's edge. By now my breath was short, and I realized I was hyperventilating, but I entered the water anyway without my usual hesitation or concern about the cold.

The moment I submerged my head in the cool water I could hear a dolphin chirping. I chirped back, and he answered in turn. I responded again, and we called back and forth to each other in this manner for quite some time. This voice contact clarified where the dolphins were, and I swam cautiously toward the sound, taking care not to disturb them in the event I got near enough for an encounter. Yet whenever I got close to the origin of the chirping, the sound seemed to shift and come from another direction. At times, I lost contact altogether and felt discouraged. Then, as soon as I would give up on seeing the dolphins and head for shore, they would make their presence known by resuming a loud chorus of chatter.

Although I'm a strong swimmer, I eventually grew tired and was reminded of others reporting how much the dolphins liked to play hide and seek. When I first heard that claim I assumed people were projecting more into the experience than was really there. Now, sensing that I was being toyed with, I laughed aloud and wondered if it was true.

My husband was also in search of the dolphins and, in his usual independent fashion, had swum out toward the horizon as far as he dared to go. From time to time he would stop to scan the ocean, looking in all directions for the elusive dolphins.

Eventually we were able to concede that neither of us had attracted them to us, and he swam over to me, where we bobbed in the water discussing whether or not to go back to shore. As we meandered slowly in the direction of the beach, we looked more carefully at the fish below and took time to point out various sea creatures to one another. In the process, we discovered that the fish and their surroundings were wonderfully exciting but that we had overlooked them in our search for dolphins.

Now we were both relaxed, feeling connected to nature and appreciating what we had right in front of us rather than chasing after what was not there. I also noticed that anytime I felt a surge of affection for the fish, they would stop swimming in the direction they were headed and turn to swim toward me instead. Whenever my heart opened further or I began to coo at them through my snorkel, they would cock their little heads to peer at me and then swim even closer. I was completely absorbed in my pleasure with this discovery and forgot for a moment about my search for the dolphins.

My husband noticed what I was doing and was equally impressed with the responsiveness of the fish. We each peered into the other's facemask and smiled.

Releasing our fear that the dolphins wouldn't come, and with a new appreciation for the beauty of the reef and fish, we were unexpectedly rewarded by three dolphins who appeared out of nowhere right below us. Then two more swam alongside us. Then three more. They glided slowly by in pairs and threes, establishing eye contact and gazing at us unwaveringly as if in a trance.

It seemed as though some extraordinary being lived behind the dolphin gaze and had come to say hello and make friends. As I gazed back through the portals of their eyes, I was enveloped by their kindness, and my body flooded with endorphins. Before long my heart was spilling over with love and my throat bubbled with laughter. I heard myself cooing and chirping at times, or whooping a "yeeha!" at others.

A new level of glee that I had never before experienced engulfed me as I realized I was being showered by the grace of God. I had heard others describe wild dolphin encounters as comparable to swimming in champagne distilled from joy, and I now understood their search for an adequate metaphor to describe such euphoria. As I surrendered to the pleasure, joy shimmered up from my soul in the form of rich laughter.

Then the dolphins slipped away as suddenly as they had arrived. My husband and I surfaced to remove our masks and grinned at each other. We agreed simultaneously that we were fully sated at long last and headed for the shore.

Once back on the beach, we decided to take a walk, and while ambling along the sand, we continued to giggle and grin as our overflow of endorphins sought outlets through every pore. On our return to our beach chairs, a group of dolphins appeared along the shoreline parallel to our walk. I reentered the water and waited on the edge of their path to see if they would connect again. They turned from the course they were on to circle me one more time and share another dose of their elixir before continuing on their way.

That afternoon we invited two young girls of Hawaiian descent to go out in a kayak with us. They were thrilled, and after some discussion, their mother consented. As soon as we had gathered ourselves into the small ocean kayak and paddled beyond the rocky shoreline, a handful of dolphins approached. They danced and jumped exuberantly all around us, while establishing playful eye contact with our youthful passengers.

Before long, a young dolphin began to jump repeatedly in front of the six-year-old seated in our bow. The more we squealed and clapped, the more often and higher he jumped. As I watched this adorably floppy baby show off his newly acquired skills, it occurred to me that this group of dolphins was composed of adolescents and babies playing amongst themselves and flirting with the children in our boat.

Just when we thought we had experienced all the bliss we could contain, the young dolphins would jump and spin again, then again, and again. Each time they leaped from the water, we would erupt into peals of joyful laughter, followed by the dolphins' intensifying their show.

The day was one of the best of my life, even though I had lived an enriched fifty years filled with extensive travel and a variety of experiences. On the other hand, the young girls with us had lived in poverty in a rural neighborhood on a small island. Yet it had been an equally special and healing day for them.

I couldn't help wondering why this connection with the dolphins had seemed so magical for each of us from such varied backgrounds. But the blessing had to have come from watching these noble beings personify the rapture of love, and their leaving us flooded with the force field of their exalted energy.

As I drifted off to sleep that night, it struck me that these dancing dolphins were coming to our shores to share their secrets about how to create the elevated state of harmony and joy they had achieved. I could also see that their second lesson had revealed the importance of learning to *play while you wait* for the things you dream about and yearn to attract.

Although these first insights had been revealed early in our connection, I had not yet grasped how much the dolphins would show me in the course of our next ten years together. It wasn't until further into the experience that I realized they were capable of showing humankind how we could embody the character traits of the higher self the dolphins possessed and, later, how to blend these traits with the steps for manifesting our desires. This combination would give us a surprisingly simple formula, not just for resolving the problems we had created but for manifesting the world of our dreams.

The dolphins were revealing the source of their magic to me and would teach me and others how to create a society filled with wisdom, love, harmony, and joy in our land-based world, just as they had done beneath the sea. By doing this, they were also showing me answers to the quest my clients and I had pursued together all those years. Yet they did this in such a simple and playful manner that I had almost missed noticing that I was being handed the keys to happiness.

Partway through the experience, I felt compelled to write about it and soon realized I was being asked to share these keys with others as well.

once the seeds of tomorrow's desires
are planted, enjoy the harvest of
    yesterday's dreams, for gratitude
and joy in present moments attract
    God's grace to you and tomorrow's
dreams draw closer while you play.

the dolphins' gifts
six qualities of the higher self

the dolphins' gifts

Giving is the highest expression of potency.
—*Erich Fromm*

Following my first connection with dolphins I was hooked on spending more time with them. And to my delight, as I indulged in this pastime over the next ten years, each experience revealed more about the source of their magic and joy.

six special traits

From the beginning, I was able to see that the dolphins' magnetism is shaped by six special traits, each woven with the others into the fabric of a dolphin's character. Each of these qualities represents a different facet of the higher self and works with the others to form the loving essence of every dolphin. This essence then merges with that of other dolphins to generate a force field of loving energy into which others are irresistibly drawn. The power of this force field not only floods the heart of each dolphin but spills into the world around him and onto those who are blessed to cross his path.

Although I was immediately blasted with a positive force and continuously bathed in their delicious energy from the moment I first met with the dolphins, only later did I understand that this special energy field is born out of their ability to consistently embody the six character traits of the higher self. I could also see by their demonstration of these loving traits how easy it would be for humans to do the same and that by copying the dolphins' model, we could create a new, more positive force field in our land-based world.

In the next six chapters I will demonstrate how the dolphins consistently embody the traits of the higher self and share them with us. I will also show how these qualities converge within the hearts of dolphins to serve as the source of their magic and joy.

six insights for manifesting our dreams

After I got to know the dolphins well enough to witness the high-level nature of their personalities, they initiated the idea that they would serve as teachers in our relationship. I readily acknowledged their qualifications and submitted to this arrangement. As a result, I was soon rewarded with a number of early insights into the mysteries of dolphin wisdom and the way to achieve the happiness I sought.

Their formula was simple and required only that my species and I learn to embody the six traits of the higher self as the dolphins do and then use their six simple and easily followed insights for manifesting our goals and the world of our dreams.

They later demonstrated that by interweaving the six traits of the higher self with the six insights for manifesting miracles, we too could raise our evolutionary development to the level the dolphins have attained.

weaving a wonder

To embark on this road toward our own more accelerated evolution, we must first become familiar with the dolphins' special traits of the higher self, which are their unwavering gifts to the world. Thus, in this section, I will introduce and describe each gift and explain how it manifests in their lives and in their interactions with others. A useful way to read about these gifts is to ask yourself how often you or the people you meet behave as the dolphins behave or offer the gifts they give as unwaveringly as they do. (Those already intimately familiar with this aspect of dolphins may wish to advance to Part 3, where I share the dolphins' formula for manifesting our dreams and show how weaving all of these parts together can lead to our own mastery and grace.)

After being exposed to the dolphins' gifts and manifesting formula, I had new hope for humanity's ability to find the happiness we seek. It became clear that by simply embodying the dolphins' gifts of character and blending them with their insights for manifesting our dreams, we could catapult our species out of the chaos we have created into a more harmonious and blissful state resembling the one the dolphins enjoy.

In Part 4, I share the dolphins' greatest gift as revealed to us in the midst of the challenge our sonar creates for them, in which they show us how we can go one step beyond manifesting our own personal desires to also create a loving and joyful world. Although this sounds like an outlandish claim, or one too difficult to actually achieve, it is in fact easier and more feasible than living the way we currently live.

unrestrained giving is the first step on
the path to liberation and joy.

CHAPTER 4

the first gift:
unfailing friendship and kindness

. . . to the dolphin alone, beyond all others, nature has granted what the best philosophers seek: friendship for no advantage.

—*Plutarch*

The quality I first noticed in the dolphins was how consistently they offer loving friendship and kindness to humankind. As I received this gift, I couldn't help noticing how easily they offer it to us and others, in contrast to the distrust and withholding of caring and kindness that has developed in human life.

This gesture of cetacean friendship can be traced as far back as the early Christians, causing some to speculate that the sign of the fish was originally a depiction of dolphins and that the head of the pope's miter looks like a dolphin's profile. It also dates back to ancient Greece, as demonstrated by the incorporation of dolphin friendship and rescue into their legends and art. And images of dolphin affiliation can be found in the cave dwellings and legends of other cultures as well. Although we initially viewed these ancient connections as enchanting myths, modern reports of dolphin friendship remove these earlier accounts from the realm of fantasy and restore them to the reality that we all can readily observe.

Dr. Horace Dobbs, one of the first to swim with individual sociable dolphins, refers to these friendly cetaceans as "ambassadors," while social psychologist Dr. Jean Houston notes that dolphins have come to our shores throughout history to meet with people prior to periods of increased enlightenment and cultural renaissance. Thus, as we enjoy these engaging encounters, we must also ask why cetaceans are revisiting our shores at this particular time to offer us their kindness.

kind friendship

Today's friendly dolphins and their larger whale cousins come to our harbors and bays throughout the world, calling and jumping and teasing and enticing until people join them for interactions, learning, and play. They also bound toward our boats in the open ocean with a glee and exuberance that clearly portend their desire for friendship. I have personally experienced these encounters with dolphins, ranging from large super-pods swimming alongside and beneath swimmers and boats to individual or small groups developing personal relationships with select human friends. I have also enjoyed more intimate interactions with both dolphins and whales, including close, personal contact and all manner of games, teasing, and high-level lessons.

Dolphins clearly let us know they are interested in our friendship by the way they bound toward us, jumping, spinning, wiggling, tail- and fin-waving or slapping, vocalizing back and forth, and glancing playfully at us. Once they arrive, they continue to leap and spin all around us, sometimes even jumping over a small boat or swimmer as they chirp and chatter with delight or engage us in flirtatious eye contact. They may even raise their bodies out of the water in a burst of joy or charm us with a back-flip or leap as high as fifteen to twenty feet into the air. I have even seen a dolphin execute a double back-flip, and I once saw a foot-long baby complete a full forward somersault.

Following this initial connection, dolphins often remain with us anywhere from five minutes to three hours or more. During this time they continue their vocalizations, wiggle with delight, roll over on their backs, do underwater somersaults, or blush with pink under their chins and underbellies as a sign that they're feeling particularly loving. Or they might swim slowly and synchronistically alongside us in the water, present their babies to us, or show us how to dive or spiral with them. Some continuously jump around us or splash one of us unexpectedly, while others bring fronds or debris to swish in front of us or pass back and forth. Most attempt to communicate in a variety of ways; respond to our vocalizations and music; imitate our sounds, smiles, and laughter; and play various games designed to tease, entertain, and teach.

Whenever a dolphin determines that he wants to connect at a deeper level, he will engage a person in more prolonged eye contact. Once this alliance is established, he locks you into his unblinking gaze and holds you there with him, heart-to-heart, for as long as five to ten minutes or more. During these encounters it feels as though a pathway between you has been opened as the dolphin drinks you into himself and claims your heart for the time you are engaged. His gaze is similar to the tender look of other wise, high-level beings as they see you as you truly are yet love you just the same. During such an interaction you are likely to feel your heart open wider as you absorb their unrestrained love and move into a higher place within yourself.

After engaging with a dolphin in one of these heart-stirring gazes, I am able to energetically recognize that particular dolphin whenever I see him again, even if I have no idea what his physical characteristics are. It is as though we have gazed beyond appearance to each other's essence. Others have suggested that we can heal the world simply by looking at each other in this deeply seeing and loving way.

pioneers of dolphin friendship

Although dolphin connections with humans reach far back in time, the current trend toward more frequent contact throughout the world did not begin until about thirty years ago.

Donald was the first of the modern individual dolphins reported to make friends. His first contact was with Dr. Horace Dobbs, who was so affected by the experience that he left his medical practice to write about their friendship and dedicate his life to dolphins. I met Dr. Dobbs at the International Cetacean Conference in Australia and learned that this elder scientist continues to view dolphins as highly intelligent and capable of profound levels of healing.

Next, Jojo, the most famous of the sociable dolphins, appeared off the coast of Provo in the British West Indies to befriend Dean Bernal, who moved from California to Provo to continue their friendship. Jojo was initially considered dangerous because he dislikes being touched and reacted aggressively to swimmers who were disrespectful of this preference. But Dean campaigned to protect Jojo from uninvited touch, and Jojo is now free to show the loving and friendly side of his personality. Jojo adores Dean, swims daily with him, and likes to bring him gifts from the sea such as crabs, fish, lobsters, shells, and assorted lost treasures, including money. Jojo is particularly fond of children and sometimes places his jaws around a child in order to tickle his or her tummy with his tongue. He is also friends with a Golden Labrador named Toffee and dives beneath the surface to nibble her paws. Jojo further enjoys passing objects back and forth and has been observed pushing a shark away from the vicinity of divers, striving as other dolphins do for a peaceful resolution when possible. Yet, when he and Dean swim together out to the deep blue water, Jojo has fought off and killed sharks when necessary to protect them. I was blessed to meet Dean and learn directly from him about his thirteen-year relationship with Jojo.

These early sociable encounters were followed by a number of other friendly dolphins who engaged in snuggling, teasing, and offering rides to their human friends. Because these early encounters were free from crowds of swimmers chasing after the dolphins, they had time to reveal their pleasure in such things as moving boat anchors, stealing bait, tangling and untangling lobster pots or bringing them to the fishermen when they were full, sneaking up from behind swimmers to startle them, pull on their flippers, and peck at their masks.

A few years before these famed individual contacts, a group of wild dolphins led by their female elder, Holey Fin, began to gather daily to meet with visitors at Monkey Mia, north of Perth in Western Australia. Lamentably, these famous dolphins are fed frozen fish, which has altered their interactions with people as well as introduced some uncharacteristic competitiveness among the dolphins. These dolphins still show up daily at Monkey Mia, now led by Nicky, the surviving daughter of Holey Fin. They often toss their fish—or a piece of seaweed—back to the people who are feeding them, perhaps in the spirit of cooperative fishing done historically with coastal-dwelling Aborigines. They also allow visitors occasionally to stroke them and are particularly attentive to children, a common dolphin trait.

Unfortunately, a number of well-known dolphin studies are based on these semi-tame dolphins, without taking into account the influence of human interaction on them, particularly the introduction of feeding. Since I have noted in my research and worldwide encounters that feeding creates significant changes in dolphin interactions with humans as well as each other, I am skeptical of any conclusions drawn from the behavior of the Monkey Mia or other semi-tame dolphins. In fact, the practice of feeding has caused so much dolphin aggression in areas off the coast of Florida that efforts are underway to legislate against this disruptive behavior.

The most prominent changes seen in semi-tame and captive dolphins include the onset of competition for food and subsequent fighting and aggression among them, even resulting in wounds. Yet I have never witnessed a single altercation in the wild and only once in ten years have I seen a free dolphin with open wounds. These were extensive enough to appear more like the work of a boat than a fellow dolphin. Moreover, the wild dolphins I have seen rarely even have the milder rake marks on their bodies from the teeth of another dolphin seen in captivity, and the marks I have seen are quite limited in number as well as very light in color and never go deep or break the skin.

accelerated dolphin friendship

Following the initial decade of sporadic encounters with individual sociable dolphins, contacts rose gradually over the next twenty years. Then about ten years ago, dolphin-initiated encounters began to rapidly accelerate and continue to rise each year. By 2000, there were seven known individual sociable dolphins and numerous pods that were meeting regularly with people all over the world.

I had my first dolphin encounter as this new wave of contacts began and was blessed to be involved before commercialism was introduced and larger crowds became a part of the experience, followed by sonar, which seemed to break much of the interspecies connection between cetaceans and people. As a result of my early contact, I was privileged to observe purely wild dolphins before their exposure to so much human interaction and the changes our more intrusive behaviors impose on human-dolphin friendship.

When I first swam with the dolphins during this uncharted period of interspecies friendship, I was continuously amazed by the variety of ways they found to share their kindness with us as well as their special brand of humor, teasing, and play.

the effect of dolphin friendship on our world

Because these loving and playful interactions evoke an accelerated ability in humans to act with friendship and kindness, it appears that dolphin friendship alone has the capacity to elevate and expand the level of human friendliness. This is explained by Ilya Prigogine's theory that once we choose a behavior such as friendliness, we not only tend to repeat our own friendliness but also influence others to do the same. This in turn results in a new pattern or template of friendship in the world.

Thus, the dolphins' practice of friendship and kindness not only offers us a model for how to make others on this planet feel welcome and loved but also triggers in us a desire to do the same. As more of us respond to this urge to be more friendly and kind, we embrace a wonderful opportunity to heal our own hearts while creating an increasingly kind and friendly world.

let loving kindness and friendship flow
from your heart toward all things
in the same way the sun shines
everywhere without discernment. not
only is this ability in dolphins the
source of their magic, the friendship
they offer makes life on this planet
considerably more joyful.

the second gift:
playful humor and joy

Humor and play are the foundation of joy.

The second gift of character I saw the dolphins consistently embody is the gift of playful humor and joy. Initially, I simply took pleasure in the delicious outfall of this wonderful quality. But over time, I fell in awe of their ability to maintain their euphoric state on such a continuous basis at a level far above what humanity has learned to achieve.

When I began to observe more carefully how dolphins were able to do this, I noticed that their joy was in part based on their enthusiasm for humor and play and a tireless commitment to fun. As a result of their dedication to happiness, not only am I moved to laughter whenever I am with them, but in their presence I am regularly transported to a state of joy.

joyful greetings

As I got to know the dolphins better, I noticed that they clearly recognize the people they have met and demonstrate excitement about our reconnecting and continuing to interact with them. For example, on days when the dolphins want to play, they may acknowledge our arrival by leaping enthusiastically into the air the moment we park our cars, sometimes adding a playful somersault or spin. Or they might make a right angle, or perhaps even a full U-turn, off the course they are on and bound shoreward toward us like old friends. In fact, this particular behavior so clearly demonstrates their recognition and desire to reconnect that newcomers often remark that the dolphins seem to know us. This open, unguarded welcome is one of the many ways that dolphins exude, from the outset, a sense of playfulness and joy in their interactions with people.

performing with love for the joy of it

After recognizing and greeting us with an exuberance that makes us feel welcomed and valued, the dolphins increase the bond of joy between us by performing a variety of stunts. For example, they love to jump and spin repeatedly near boats or swimmers, eliciting an element of surprise each time they get a bit closer or are able to leap yet one more time into the air. Some add to this merry experience by establishing eye contact or vocalizing while in the middle of their jumps or doing an unusual landing, perhaps splashing a member of our group.

The agile babies and adolescents also enjoy showing off their jumps, particularly their "air dolphin" style of "flying" in which they hang in the air while moving forward for extended periods of time as if imitating basketball superstar Michael Jordan. The dolphins possessing this skill seem to take particular pleasure in the applause and hysteria it creates in their audience, and we can see their bodies shudder in mid-air with the exhilaration they feel.

I witnessed a particularly memorable cetacean performance in Mexico when a young whale calf jumped repeatedly to the applause of appreciative onlookers. With each jump he managed to hang an extra moment in the air while holding prolonged eye contact with us as his pectorals flopped adorably to the side. It seemed as if he was making sure not to miss a moment of our pleasure. Just when we thought he couldn't possibly continue, he would make yet another jump, reaching a total of fifteen in all. This calf was clearly stage-struck, and I felt as though my applause had been part of shaping one of the renowned Mexican "friendlies" or "las amistosas."

Another special performance involved a group of five baby dolphins on the Big Island of Hawaii. They were independently riding without their mothers in the bow wave of our boat, which had slowed down while we were deciding what to do next. I had never seen such young dolphins solo before, so I was surprised when this group was allowed to ride all by themselves. These babies seemed quite pleased with themselves and became extra wiggly whenever our crowd exclaimed over their beauty and youth.

One was adept enough to jump periodically, which drew great cheers from our crowd. Seemingly struck by our applause, he proceeded to jump higher and higher with each passing minute as we hooted and hollered "hana hou" (Hawaiian for "encore"). This adorable young dolphin clearly relished the delight and laughter of his happy audience and to our amazement kept jumping. One of his buddies got the idea and joined in, then another tried it as well. Only the first jumper was able to coordinate his jumps with glances at the people and toward the end included some prolonged, flirty looks and a little kick to his jumps, adding to our laughter and joy.

Eventually our captain began to speed our boat up slightly, causing the babies to drop out one by one. The talented jumper was the last to leave and, as he did, surprised us all by leaping a full ten feet into the air, sneaking a self-satisfied peek at us from the top of his jump. When this elicited another eruption of hollers, he did it again, then again and again as he danced his way out of our bow wave, raising the level of our cheers a few more decibels. He was the best of the aspiring "Michael Jordans" I have seen to date and seemed to take enormous pleasure in provoking our joy as his skills developed before our eyes. He was clearly a stage-struck "amistosa."

After this baby had completed his performance, an adolescent leaped twenty feet out of the water to bring down the house. The adolescent then continued to make twenty-foot jumps repeatedly as we screamed "hana hou" louder and louder with each jump. We were sure he couldn't do another, so we were as surprised as we were delighted each time he surfaced one more time. This lasted for about twenty more jumps as the pod moved away from our boat toward the horizon.

Many dolphins appear to delight in being photographed and not only hang out in front of a still or video camera but often slow down to peek into the lens and pose or perform a variety of activities. In fact, this is so consistent that I often suggest to newcomers that they swim near the photographers, since they are more likely to see dolphins that way. This behavior not only suggests that the dolphins understand their photo is being taken but is yet another way of bringing pleasure to the people filming them.

One day I noticed a man absorbed in taking video shots of some fish in the bay. I commented with a laugh to my friend as we passed him on our way out that the dolphins would probably show up, since he had such a good camera. Later, while on our way back to shore, we passed this man again in time to see a couple of dolphins sneak up behind him and startle him by appearing unexpectedly in front of his lens. We all had a good laugh over this typically dolphin-like encounter, and I couldn't help but wonder if their timing was designed to include us in the humor of this moment as well.

A national television film crew visiting Tonga benefited from this cetacean interest in photography when a group of whales performed their exhilarating spiral dance, which looks like a giant rose opening underwater, in front of the cameras. Even these seasoned photographers were "blown away" by the wonder of this beautiful ballet. I have seen other footage of individual whales provoking joy with their unexpected grace by spinning upright underwater, leading each spin with their heads, followed by their bodies as their pectoral fins flow gracefully behind their spin in the same style a ballerina might use for a series of pirouettes.

imitating for fun

Dolphins further provoke our joy by doing such things as imitating or teasing us in a variety of humorous ways. For example, one day as I swam in the bay I could hear a radio on the beach strumming out a Hawaiian tune, and I began to do a hula in the water. Before long, a dolphin appeared and swam beneath me, clearly imitating my dance by swaying his body back and forth in a sideways motion quite awkward for dolphins. I cheered and laughed when I noticed this, and he in turn opened his mouth in mock laughter and held it in that position while continuing to sway his body back and forth.

Another time a group of dolphins arrived and were swimming directly beneath me in a slow, gliding motion while keeping pace with my steady but gentle kicking as I moved along directly above them. When I switched to a dolphin kick, a dolphin beneath me did a humorous imitation of my awkward attempt to move like a dolphin. Then remembering that it would be as difficult for him to duplicate a side-to-side hula motion as it was for me to do a dolphin kick, I thought, "How about a hula?" and began to sway my hips from side-to-side above him. He immediately began to mimic my hula as well as he could and then returned to his imitation of my awkward dolphin kick. In addition to mirroring my antics, this dolphin, who was swimming directly beneath me, never used his eyes to see what I was doing—he had clearly picked me up with his sonar.

the play of bow-riding

Dolphins further connect with people in the spirit of exuberance and joy whenever they ride the bow waves of our boats or surf in the waves made by the boat's wake. During bow-riding there is a special exchange between the dolphins and people, as we give them the gift of our wave and they return it with the essence of their joyful play. I have watched bow-riding dolphins generate this feeling of joy by glancing at us, taking turns on cue, and even nuzzling each other while maintaining their weaving pattern in the boat's wave.

Often a dolphin will flirt with a person on board while bow-riding, and I always feel honored when I am the one selected. Once when my friend Sue and I were enjoying a group of dolphins playing in the bow wave of our boat, Sue noticed that one of them had a V-cut in the center of his dorsal fin and decided to name him

"Notch," which he seemed to enjoy. When she later asked him aloud if there were other dolphins with notches in their fins, "Notch" immediately left his place at the front of the bow. As I looked at her to say, "I guess not," he returned with a fellow dolphin sporting a notch on his dorsal as well. Sue and I squealed with delight as the twin "Notches" then rode our wave in tandem, tilted slightly to the side so that we could more clearly see their notches as they gazed up at us with pleasure in our recognition of what had just transpired.

One man crewing on a boat returning from New Zealand to Australia had a special encounter when he went topside for a cigarette at 3 a.m. To his surprise, he found dolphins riding the bow wave of this large vessel. Not only was it interesting for him to see these exhilarated dolphins participating in a joyful ride in the middle of the night, but the bow wave was saturated with the blue luminescence of phosphorous, making the sight even more magical.

Although I had already witnessed a great deal of bow-riding, I was fascinated when hundreds of common dolphins suddenly emerged from the Sea of Cortez simultaneously to bound joyfully toward us with a sense of glee. When they arrived, they made a sharp U-turn and followed alongside our boat for the next half hour as they took turns riding our bow wave. Because hundreds of dolphins had surfaced for this ride, their turns were brief as they easily cooperated without any struggle to accommodate each dolphin who wanted a ride. When their group was finished, the last dolphin signed off, as they do throughout the world, with a few extra jumps accompanied by a final glance and a chirp to thank us for the gift of the wave and to evoke a final fragment of pleasure from our group.

surfing for fun and friendship

There have been a number of recent reports of dolphins approaching surfers at such places as Zuma, Malibu, and other beaches in California in order to play together and enjoy interspecies surfing. Dolphins have also been sighted riding waves with surfers in

Australia and were recently observed out-performing the board-surfers in some unusually large waves.

More recently, a newsclip showed a pod of dolphins surfing alongside contestants during the 1998 summer surfing contest in South Africa. As I watched this clip and saw how easily the dolphins had gained international coverage, I wondered if they were escalating their program for connecting with humanity and winning our hearts through this delightful surprise performance in the spotlight.

This would match the dolphins' capacity for seizing the moment to bring joy to humanity, even though a few months before, the U.S. Navy had begun an underwater sonar testing program that not only appeared to be disruptive to the peace and health of dolphins and whales but, if continued, could be potentially harmful to their well-being and survival. Responding to this unconscionable act with the gift of joy would be very dolphin-like. It also matches Jacques Cousteau's belief after years of diving with dolphins that they have the capacity for irony.

the play of the trickster

In support of Cousteau's observation, I too have noticed that the most interesting aspect of dolphin humor is their grasp of irony and the way they weave it into their role as tricksters.

A trickster's approach to humor and play is an art form steeped in teasing and the element of surprise. When timed correctly, this form of humor results in gleeful levels of joy, and dolphins are masters of the art. Their success as tricksters lies in their uncanny ability to create humorous disruptions to expected outcomes. Since our addiction to order and predictable results stands in the way of our lightness and joy, dolphins constantly work to break this down whenever they are with people. They do this by setting us up for one expectation and then giving us another. Once they get us laughing at ourselves, our hearts become lighter and life flows easier.

One of the ways captive dolphins play the role of the trickster is by creating opportunities to gain unexpected control over their captors, even if only by refusing or delaying compliance.

Sometimes they are even able to reverse roles with their trainers and assume the position of leader. For example, one dolphin enjoyed starting the hotel's dolphin show prematurely whenever an unusually long-winded young trainer was on duty. As this trainer stood with his back to the dolphins and droned on to his captive audience, Keola would engage in a variety of antics that got people laughing. Whenever the trainer would turn around to see what was happening, Keola would stop, arousing more laughter, and then begin again when the trainer returned to his talk. Keola had found a way to help everyone out by bringing unexpected humor and joy to this otherwise boring situation.

In addition to trumping their trainers, dolphins are known for luring visitors close to them with an implied promise of a special connection, and then splashing them with a wall of water. As the wet victim recovers, the trickster dolphin looks playfully into the soaking victim's eyes with the glow of a smile erupting from within, literally transforming the shape of the dolphin's malleable face into a look of rapture.

I have also experienced the honor of being drenched in this way by a captive dolphin as well as a gray whale in the San Ignacio Lagoon in Baja California, Mexico. After flirting with me, the frisky whale filled his blowhole with water, fixed his twinkly eye on me, and swam deliberately in my direction. When he then released the entire drenching contents of his saved water on me, everyone on our boat laughed uproariously. Fortunately when a cetacean douses you in this manner, it is viewed as a sign of playful affection and is one of the ways the famed Keiko liked to interact with his trainers in Oregon before his release and ultimate death.

A game wild dolphins particularly enjoy is taunting swimmers by playing hide-and-seek. I have been teased many times by dolphins repeatedly jumping and dancing on the water's surface to lure our group into the water, then disappearing and becoming silent once we are in. When at last we give up and head for shore, the dolphins break into a loud chorus of chatter and squeals, revealing that they are right behind us, as if to promise that they are now ready to play. But when we turn back to join them, the dolphins fall silent again and cannot be found. Sometimes this game goes on for hours, thoroughly exhausting the swimmers. Yet even though we are pooped, we cannot help joining the other duped swimmers in laughter at this exquisitely mischievous humor. Interestingly, this game always serves as a catalyst for the swimmers and beachgoers to become bonded as well, something the dolphins often make clear in a variety of ways that they like very much and want us to do.

Once, after playing hide-and-seek for over an hour, my son flopped exhausted on the beach and announced that he would not fall for the dolphins' attempt to lure him back into the water again. He felt sure they had no intention of allowing a connection that day and decided to outsmart them by sitting firmly on the shore. Besides, he asserted, he was enjoying watching their jumping from the beach as much as striving for a personal connection. The minute he made this proclamation, the dolphins began to jump and spin from a spot unusually close to the shoreline. My daughter-in-law and I looked at each other and laughed as we surrendered to the bait and exhaustedly pulled our gear back on. My son sat firmly on the sand as we entered the water for a very special encounter. My daughter-in-law and I were just getting to know each other, and this afforded us a delightfully bonded moment as we held hands and cried in response to the extra dose of love being blasted our way, probably in acknowledgment and support of our bonding. As we headed back for shore, we bumped into my son laughing at himself for being in the water right behind us. Usually quite determined, he had not succeeded in resisting the dolphins' allure, yet they managed to elude their "faithless friend," and he did not swim with them that day.

Another game the dolphins enjoy is the leaf game, which they initiate by using leaves and fronds or some other debris such as garbage bags to exchange back and forth with each other or with us. They dive fairly deep with their object before dropping it and then look up at a designated swimmer to dive down after it. With each pass, the dolphin may take the object slightly deeper, typically challenging us to stretch ourselves a bit more. In other cases, they interject an unexpected element either by not giving up the object after one of us has passed it to them or by letting it go and scrambling to reclaim it before we have a chance to get it.

Dolphins behave in playful ways with other species as well. For example, one dolphin was seen placing a piece of squid outside the home of a grouper fish, but when the fish came out to claim the squid, the dolphin snatched it away. They have also been seen sneaking up on pelicans to steal a few tail feathers and rolling turtles over a few times as they are swimming along, perhaps to share the pleasures of spinning that the dolphins themselves enjoy.

finding joy through choosing play

Initially I found it hard to pull away from the piles on my desk to simply go frolic and play with dolphins in this undirected and frivolous way. I felt guilty and concerned that I would get behind on my important projects and deadlines. Yet each time I resisted going on a day I felt called, I later learned that something special had happened.

As a result, I learned the hard way to place more value on the joy of humor and play, and over time it got easier to leave my desk in favor of the joy I experienced at the bay. I also noticed that anytime I surrendered to the dolphins' call to play, when I returned home, I was able to finish my work with much greater ease. Eventually I could see the error of my habit of striving to complete work before allotting time to play. And the more I surrendered to play, the more I was reminded of the happiness of my youth before work had become such a large part of my life.

I was continually amazed by how simple the dolphins' life was and often chided them about their ease in spending the day just playing since they had no mortgage to pay. Yet I soon saw that life could be similarly light for humans if we would commit to more simplicity and surrender our schedules and work to more time for the sheer joy of laughter and play.

I was beginning to see that by showing me their capacity for simple friendship and kindness, laced with joyful humor and play, the dolphins had already given me two extraordinary gifts. It became clear that if I and members of my species would embody these qualities as fully as the dolphins have, our lives would be transformed in deep and meaningful ways.

Yet, in spite of the profundity of this idea, there were even more of the dolphins' gifts to come.

put humor and play first on your
agenda, for this is the source of the joy
we work so hard to attain
while the dolphins simply play.

the third gift:

harmony among themselves and others

Blending hearts leads to harmony.

The dolphins' third gift is the choice they make to behave in a consistently harmonious manner and to share their harmony with us, even when we abuse it. By contrast, we are regularly out of harmony in our interactions with ourselves and others and must spend much of our energy and time repairing the discord we create.

wild harmony

Because I was among the early pioneers to swim with dolphins in the open ocean, I was initially unsure of what their actions meant or if they would behave aggressively toward me. I had read they were among the strongest animals on earth and were not only dominant over sharks but could kill us with a thrust of their tails. I had also heard accounts of their aggression in captivity and of people who had been seriously injured in swim programs. And I had learned from studies of wild dolphins highly exposed to humans, particularly if fed by them, of their capacity for aggression. I had further been warned that repeated tail slapping indicates unhappiness and that a dolphin swimming directly at a swimmer while nodding his head or clapping his jaw is forcefully defining his territorial boundaries or preparing to ram the intruder.

As a result, when the wild dolphins first got close enough for me to see their large size and hear the sound of their loud, rhythmic breathing, I felt duly intimidated. I was out in deep, open water several hundred yards from the shore, and although I was counting on a friendly meeting between species, I had no assurance I would get one. Yet, in spite of my concerns, I continued to yearn for the experience of swimming with wild dolphins. And so I took the risk.

When the dolphins finally appeared beside me during my first encounter, I was initially startled and my heart began to pound. But elation soon flooded my entire being, and I was surprised by how quickly their presence quelled my fears. Not only did they offer peaceful friendship as I had hoped, but their slow swimming, meditative tempo, and languid gazes all served as pacifiers that helped to calm my concerns. With this approach, they began our friendship in the context of harmony.

dancing with the dolphins

Even after making this reassuringly peaceful connection with the dolphins, I felt appropriately subdued as an outsider in their world. Consequently I remained passive and watched to see what they would do next rather than interrupt their approach with ideas of my own, based on images from fantasy films and captive dolphin shows.

This allowed both space and time for the dolphins to initiate the many elements of our experience strictly on their terms. What they chose for our first interaction was to circle slowly around me and draw increasingly closer at their own pace. Because I waited for them to take the initiative and did not chase after them as most swimmers do, they were able to gradually get near enough for me to see them at close range. Calmed by their movements, I was able to feel their loving yet powerful energy grow increasingly stronger the closer they drew, and once our connection was comfortably in place, we enjoyed gazing at each other as they continued slowly to circle me in a harmonious embrace.

One of the larger males then broke away from the others to draw even with me. Once his sizable body was within a few feet of me, he looked deeply into my eyes and held this connection by locking me into a prolonged gaze. As with the captive dolphins, I could feel him pull me through the portals of his eyes and into his heart. Yet with him, the pull felt so strong that even when I snuffed some water through my snorkel and was choking a bit, I didn't want to break the connection.

Then, as a result of some unseen but viscerally felt signal, I knew to swim in slow motion, side-by-side, on a parallel course with him. The other dolphins continued to swim along as well, but they remained in the background of the experience, while the large dolphin served as my escort.

Following this encounter, I could always identify this dolphin by his essence rather than his markings and by my recollection of the eye-to-eye contact and heart-to-heart connection he continued to establish between us. Once we connected, it felt as though I was receiving instructions from him on what to do next. These seemed to come from his entire being—his mind, heart, eyes, and even his body and skin. My years as a counselor helped me to listen in the sensitive, intuitive way needed to grasp the quiet essence of his subtle, energetic instructions. Thus, the more I was still and listened carefully with my heart to what was happening between us, the clearer his communication became.

As a result, I could feel this guide dolphin entrain or conform to my movements while entraining me to his as he firmly held heart and eye contact between us. It felt like a dance with the most enchanting partner imaginable, and I was always overcome with joy after these ballets. Following our first dance together, I began to refer to this dolphin as "my dolphin guide," although I also thought of him as "the prince."

I later learned from this lead dolphin how to do slow-motion dives and turns, either alone with him or with a group of his dolphin friends. Again, during these lessons it felt as though he was signaling me with projected mental and body cues, letting me know that he would be moving right, or left, or diving, or turning. Whenever other dolphins were present, they seemed to know which way he would move as well, so that all of our movements were as synchronized as a water ballet.

Whenever I swam alongside the dolphins in this parallel manner, I could see and feel them shift down to a slower speed that seemed to match the tempo of an eighth note, then a quarter note, and finally a half or whole note as measured in music. This shift to an increasingly slower cadence not only accommodated my slower swimming pace but created the feeling that I was following the dolphins into an alpha brain wave or meditative state. When I spent longer periods with them, this state seemed to go even deeper into the slower theta brain waves, which I assumed accounted for the loss of time orientation I felt in which three hours might seem like forty-five minutes.

Ten years after first noticing this time warp, I came across a study in which people measured on an EEG after spending time with dolphins not only revealed alpha states as expected but showed lower theta states similar to those of people under anesthesia. These results could account for the deep levels of peace and harmony such swimmers attain as well as the time distortion so often reported.

Each time I have danced with the dolphins in this mesmerizing way, I have personally experienced how their entraining to each other's loving and peaceful meditative states contributes to the achievement of so much harmony between them.

bonded connections and harmony

Although bonded hearts are the greatest predictor of harmony in a culture, our society is constructed around our competition for material things, how many of those objects we can afford, and who can obtain the most goods. This causes us not only to feel separated from each other and develop in jealous, competitive, and self-serving ways, but also to create serious breaks in our bonds with our families and children as we pursue our material goals. By contrast, the dolphins spend their time swimming meditatively and breathing rhythmically together in family groups while participating as a pod in survival and leisure activities as well as pursuits of the higher self.

In addition to early breaks in our family bonds, humans often promote independence as a prerequisite to maturity and encourage adolescents to break even further from their families in order to achieve this. By contrast, interdependence and connection are highly valued in the dolphin society and serve as the glue that bonds them in a loving societal partnership. As a result, dolphins are almost always seen in groups of two or more, and interacting closely with their families, often touching or holding fins as they travel. By contrast, humans often feel disconnected from others and lose their comfort with touch, then search for the love of one special person to fill their emptiness. Yet this approach ultimately results in feelings of isolation and sadness or anger, which gets expressed as depression or acted out as violence in our homes, schools, and streets.

achieving cooperative synergy

As a result of noticing these differences between dolphins and humans, I began to pay closer attention to see if I could uncover additional secrets as to how dolphins live with such high levels of harmony and peace. As I sharpened my focus, a number of things caught my attention.

First, I noticed that the dolphins' breaths, which take place consciously rather than automatically as ours do, are often synchronized during extended periods of swimming as a group. In addition, they regularly gaze at each other in the same way they gaze at us and closely coordinate their movements while swimming in unison. These activities seem to result in deep and steady entrainment to one another, which in turn serves as the foundation for their harmonious patterns of behavior. Interestingly, the hotel dolphins, several of whom were captured following a few years with their families in the wild, continue to engage in this ritual of circling their lagoon together for about an hour each morning before starting their day.

In addition to this group-bonding and meditative time, group structures for playing, jumping, diving, communicating, singing, caring, stroking, lovemaking, birthing, baby-tending, grieving, fishing, and protecting are so connected and harmonious that they serve both the group and individual needs of free dolphins simultaneously.

bonds with family as primary

Although humans speak a great deal about the value of family, we tend to keep our children separate from our adult world by leaving them with caregivers, in school, or endlessly watching TV or playing video games. As a result, not only do our children feel isolated, but we also lose our opportunity to communicate, play, or pass our knowledge and wisdom on to them. By contrast, dolphins actually live as though family comes first and spend most of their time in family groups, while touching, playing and surviving together. In fact, their family bonds are so strong that if one or two dolphins find a way to escape a fishing net, they won't leave unless the rest of their pod is also able to get free. Similarly, if a baby dolphin becomes trapped, his mother will attempt to enter the net in order to die with him. Moreover, mass strandings are thought by some to be the result of an entire pod following a few unhealthy members to their death.

The intensity of these bonds was further demonstrated during the U.S. Navy's sonar testing in Hawaii in the spring of 1998, when researchers observed as large pods huddled together holding their heads above water during the tests. Another group later watched helplessly for five hours as a whale calf, who apparently became disoriented during the testing, breached over two hundred times and pectoral-slapped over six hundred times before the sun set on his desperate effort to reconnect with his mother. Since abandonment is rarely seen in cetacean populations, it was distressing to find this calf and others who had been separated from their groups struggling in Hawaiian waters during these tests.

We can see from these examples how genuinely important family bonds are to dolphins and why our capturing and separating them from their pods in the wild, and then again after they are in captivity, is so painful for them. This also explains why Iwa, the special healing dolphin, became so depressed after a move that separated her from the dolphin family she had adopted for so many years while at the hotel.

I happened to visit Iwa on the day she was being transferred and learned that she was pregnant. When I told her aloud in front of several family members that I would visit her new baby at the park when it was born, Iwa turned over and raised her white belly all the way to the surface of the lagoon, while gazing into my eyes. She remained there for several minutes, continuing to hold eye contact with me, as her belly flushed with pink, while my family and I expressed our amazement at how she obviously understood and appreciated my comment about something so precious to her.

Many months later, when I went to visit Iwa and her baby, I discovered that they were in an overcrowded tank. Iwa initially greeted me like her long-lost hope and rushed to the side of the pool and stood upright before me in this honoring position while holding steady eye contact for most of my twenty-minute visit. When I asked where her baby was she dove underwater, swam to the far end of the tank, and returned with her young calf, who also greeted me in the upright position, as did Hoku, her older offspring who had been moved there earlier. Everyone watching these two events confessed their amazement, and it felt as though Iwa was doing her part to honor her bonds with old friends while in her new environment.

Yet, following this encounter and my inability to help Iwa as I had telepathically promised, she refused to even look at me during subsequent visits, though I caught her stealing vacant glances from afar. It broke my heart to see this wonderful dolphin exhibit such deep depression and loss of hope in holding the bonds that are so important to a dolphin's very existence. Iwa's plight served as one of the motivators for me to continue to write this book when, on occasion, it became a challenge to do so.

Happily, years later, Iwa was selected as nursemaid to a whale calf rescued during the sonar testing period and, following this duty, was put in a tank with other females she could befriend. Thus, her situation has greatly improved, and she now greets me fondly whenever I visit.

the bond of community birthing

When dolphin midwives sense the birth of a baby, they gather around to guard the mother and attend the birth. They later help to care for the baby by gathering to create a play area within which the newborn is protected and can move about freely. Babies not only stay with their devoted mothers from three to six years, but also return to their family group after starting their own families.

When invited, dolphins are also willing to assist with human births, and they attended a number of these in the 1960s with Igor Tjarkovsky in the Black Sea in Russia, as well as in Israel and other locations. It seems that these dolphins sensed when a human birth was due and showed up, remaining in the area during the process. When the birth was complete, these dolphins were known to swim with the newborn and the mother prior to the cord being cut, requiring the baby to breathe on his own. Russian studies show that human babies birthed with dolphins in attendance are not only calmer and stronger, but also brighter and more verbal.

bonding with humanity through babies

Dolphins not only like to connect with our children but also enjoy sharing their own babies with non-intrusive swimmers and people they've grown to love. On those occasions when I have been the recipient of this honor, I have noted that most newborns being presented swim in the middle of a group of adults, although several mothers have seemed to trust me enough to present their babies to me—sometimes while nursing them—without the protective formation of the larger group. The baby seems very aware of being presented and usually wiggles his floppy, sometimes wrinkly, new body with excitement and pleasure while holding brief glimpses of eye contact with his audience. These babies often blush with pink as dolphins do when they are feeling particularly loved and loving. Presenting their highly valued babies to us in this manner is one of the ways dolphins deepen their bonds with their human friends.

A swimmer who is even more fully trusted may be shown a birth, although this is very rare and something I have not yet seen documented by pictures. Although I have been blessed by the opportunity to view a number of brand-new and nursing babies and the beginning of a birth, I have not yet witnessed a full birth. My friend Joan Ocean (*Dolphins into the Future*, 1997), who has swum almost daily with dolphins for more than fifteen years, has witnessed a number of births, and is always careful to remain in the background as an observer without interfering.

connection through touch

In addition to being sexually active, dolphins enjoy touching each other in friendship as they swim, stroking and scratching one another with their dorsals, fins, mouths, and tails, and swimming belly-to-belly while touching flippers as if holding hands. It is always a joy to watch bonded dolphins swim synchronistically together in pairs and threesomes or more, as well as dive, twist, turn, and even jump together on an invisible cue as if they had trained with the Bolshoi Ballet.

discipline in service of harmony

To establish discipline and boundaries with their young as well as with others, wild dolphins generally use posturing gestures such as tail-slapping, tooth-raking, or face-to-face head-nodding, which may culminate in jaw-clapping. It's interesting to note how mild these boundary-marking and disciplinary acts are in view of the fact that dolphins are among the world's strongest animals and are able to dominate or even kill sharks if necessary.

I have been in the water when dolphins began to tail-slap with an energy that provided a clear signal to swimmers who were chasing them to back off. I was also approached aggressively on one occasion without understanding why, and although it felt more like a warning than a threat to my safety, I quickly withdrew. Unfortunately, many swimmers fail to read these messages correctly and remain in the area or even continue to inappropriately pursue. Although dolphins and whales generally demonstrate a great deal of restraint and patience with human rudeness, people have been reported to be seriously hurt and even killed by cetaceans who do react to the intrusive and aggressive behavior of humans. Thus, not heeding fair warnings from dolphins and whales is risky business.

When dolphins and whales can't get the surrender they need from their young, they may hold them underwater for longer than is comfortable in order to reestablish their dominance and parental authority. Although I don't believe in such drastic measures, as a parenting specialist (*Parachutes for Parents*, 1997), I do understand how essential parental authority is to good parenting and a harmonious society. Yet our species is not as clear about the need to gain surrender to societal rules from our young and allows them to regularly choose transgressions against others. This boundary-breaking pattern has become a repeating template among humans, which causes serious disruptions in our children's development and, ultimately, to our society and world.

In contrast to our permissiveness, dolphins and whales hold crisply and clearly to their boundaries. In fact, this clarity was applied to a woman off Maui who initiated an overly forward approach to a whale and, without invitation, vigorously rubbed his back. The whale responded to this inappropriate transgression by taking the woman's ankle gently between his teeth and pulling her about thirty-five feet underwater until she thought she would expire. The whale then gently nudged the woman back to the surface in the same manner he might surface a calf being disciplined.

A videotape of this encounter taken by the woman's companion was aired on national television.

the harmony of compassion

Another way the dolphins share the harmony of their hearts with each other and the world is through their capacity for compassion. I first noticed this at a time when I felt deeply saddened by some news I had received. Rather than tease me as they often do or ignore me as they do when my energy is self-pitying, the dolphins seemed to sense the genuine quality of my mood and understood my deep feelings of loss. As a result they came in very close to shore that day and remained bobbing quietly in front of my parked car as I cried. Once my tears were spent and I felt calm and peaceful again, the dolphins quietly left.

In another instance, a friend took her daughters to swim with the dolphins following her mother's death and was surprised to find them seeming to wait in the shallow part of the bay for her party to arrive. When she and her girls entered the water, the dolphins gathered around and proceeded to circle them silently for the next forty-five minutes, much in the way they are reported to do when grieving their own dead.

In addition to offering us such kind compassion, dolphins offer each other deep levels of caring and have been seen carrying sick or dying dolphins for days, without stopping, until their assistance is no longer required.

Mother dolphins are also known to carry their dead calves along the surface anywhere from several hours to several days, while accompanied by their pods, who patiently remain with them for as long as she needs them—i.e., until the calf disintegrates or the mother is ready to release it and deposit it at a shallow shoreline. An Australian fisherman respectfully joined one of these corteges for over an hour and then watched the group stop to communicate before the mother proceeded alone to the beach with her dead infant. When she got to a shallow area, she released her baby and, after nuzzling his head with hers several times, slowly returned to her family group. Following these funerals, such mothers appear to experience extended periods of grief and depression similar to that of human mothers.

Adult dolphins are also carried and grieved. One female elder was carried dramatically for days along the Ventura and Malibu coastline for all to see before being released at Manhattan Beach. There were many reports of this sight, several newspaper articles, and a good deal of speculation as to its meaning. But a sensitive young man who got closest to this cortege while on his surfboard felt they were acting as one intelligent species trying to let another intelligent species know something was wrong. Members from a group attending a meeting about protecting dolphins and whales also saw this procession go by and wondered if the timing was purposeful.

In this regard, it appears that cetaceans not only offer us compassion but seek ours as well, perhaps to move us to right action. This may be why the whale calf breaching in desperation following the sonar tests did so in front of a group of researchers or why a dolphin once showed me his wounds that seemed to have come from a boat propeller. It may be why the captive dolphin sent us his pain and why so many dolphins bring us garbage from the sea, or why Laukani showed me her red tongue and Keola allowed me to fuss over a particularly deep wound he had incurred in captivity. It may be why Iwa showed me her depression and a gray whale deliberately showed a Makah hunter her harpoon scars by pulling alongside his boat to present her newborn calf to him. And it may even explain why dolphins and whales strand themselves on our beaches when they are dying from such things as pollution or exposure to sonar.

the bonds of rescue and protection

Whenever something threatens a pod, the group responds as a harmonious unit by huddling together with males on the outside, mothers forming the next layer, and the young in the middle.

In the service of interspecies harmony, dolphins extend protection and rescue to other species as well. I experienced this kindness one day when a group of dolphins were playing in the bow wave of our kayak. We were enjoying sharing this experience with a friend and failed to pay attention to the fact that we were gradually heading out to sea. Just as we felt the wind picking up and noticed how far we had gone, the dolphins dove underwater and left as though releasing us to return to shore. Although our guest was not a strong paddler, she and my ex-husband teamed up to get us to shore. Initially this seemed to work as the dolphins playfully made their way to the beach, but after a while I began to feel uneasy about the slowness of our progress.

Then, quite unexpectedly, I felt a flash of alarm go through my body, and I no longer felt safe. Within moments, two large dolphins appeared on each side of our kayak in a position that made them look like sentries preparing to serve as escorts. They were all business and swam in unison out ahead of our kayak toward the bay, indicating a new direction to take, and then circled back alongside our kayak to pick us up before swimming toward shore again. Their affect was one of seriousness rather than play, and our guest picked up their shift and surrendered her paddle to me.

For the next half hour, we were able to inch toward shore as we paddled steadily against an increasingly strong current and wind, while the dolphins swam with a steady rhythm by our side. Once we were out of danger, I was able to relax again, at which moment the dolphins leaped simultaneously out of the water, engaged me in eye contact as they turned together in mid-air and dove under the water to return to their pod. I wasn't sure if my feelings of alarm had called these guard dolphins to our aid, if a signal from them had alarmed me, or if the two were interactive and simultaneous. In any case, I knew that I had been engaged in an intense nonverbal communication with the dolphins that day that resembled interactions I had had with my children when they were young and urgently needed my help.

On another occasion, the dolphins were in the bay making strange noises but would not show themselves to any of us or get close enough to play. In due time, we began to notice an energy of tension in the water and sensed the dolphins were warning us about a shark. Once we verbalized this, we all quickly headed for shore. Sure enough, a lifeguard arrived within the next fifteen minutes to warn that a shark had been sighted at a beach west of ours and was swimming our way.

Ancient stories about dolphins offering friendship or providing this kind of protection and rescue were initially believed to be myths. However, as increasing numbers of similar stories surface today, this view is being reassessed. One of the more dramatic of these modern rescues involves a friend of mine who had a diving accident and was stranded in rough, shark-infested waters for a number of hours. While she waited limp in her life vest, yearning to be rescued and reunited with her young child, a group of dolphins arrived and circled her throughout her entire ordeal. Not only did they protect her from sharks, their presence also kept her calm and able to persevere. In addition, the dolphins' ability to send out an alarm as they had with me during our kayak experience may have enabled her rescuers to locate her as well. Interestingly, the degree of her recovery from the bends, given the significant delay in her treatment, was unexpected, and she defied her doctor's prediction that she would never walk again.

In the year 2000, the Cuban child, Elian Gonzalez, was known chiefly for the struggle between two families and two countries over who would shelter and care for him. But a sub-story that barely made the news was of his dramatic rescue by dolphins. I happened to be in touch with Cuban reporters from *The Miami Herald* during this period, who shared the details of this story, some of which Elian described to Diane Sawyer on national television.

The first thing Elian told the fishermen who picked him up was that dolphins circled his inner tube the entire time he was in the ocean and held him up when he would fall asleep and begin to slip through the tube. He also said that they chased off sharks and directed his tube toward the shore. Elian was very clear that it was the dolphins who had saved his life, and he wanted to talk about it.

Twelve adults did not survive this ordeal, and those who did were hospitalized for several days for overexposure, sunburn, and exhaustion—but Elian did not suffer the same physical distress. I suspect that the healing abilities of the dolphins helped in this regard, and I've often wondered if their sending sonar pings on areas of his body, comparable to the tapping points used in today's "energy therapies," helped him manage the double trauma of losing his mother and being in the ocean by himself for so long.

Another interesting point is that members of the Cuban community felt that Elian might be the boy in the Cuban legend about a boy who would come out of the sea accompanied by dolphins and bring good luck to the country where he lived.

the harmonizing gift of healing

I had read extensively about the dolphins' ability to heal human depression, autism, retardation, attention-deficit hyperactivity disorder, and autoimmune and terminal diseases, as well as helping with spinal cord injuries and many other physical and emotional problems. I initially assumed these claims to be excessive, but later learned that studies consistently support them and much more. Yet, even after reviewing the research, it wasn't until I had my own personal experience that I truly understood the magic of their healing power.

Following an ear infection many years earlier, I had developed a problem with water rushing into my left ear whenever I submerged my head in water. This invariably led to an ear infection and resulted in my needing to wear putty earplugs for swimming in order to avoid further problems. Soon after entering the water at the bay one day when I was still hoping to connect with the dolphins, I felt a tapping sensation on the left side of my face in front of my ear. I didn't understand what this odd sensation might be and kept touching my face as I puzzled over it. Meanwhile both of the putty plugs began to ooze out of my ears in spite of my efforts to push them back. This had never happened before, and I was both bewildered and dismayed since I didn't want to be distracted in the event the dolphins showed up.

Eventually, I sensed a mental impulse that I was supposed to leave the plugs out and that the ear problem was "over." I was afraid to accept this idea and go without the plugs. Yet the idea persisted and repeated in my mind. Besides, I couldn't keep the plugs in anyway and could hear some squealing in the distance, which I thought might be dolphins. Thus, I decided to test the message and cautiously lowered my head underwater without the plugs, cringing and waiting for water to rush into my left ear as it always did. But this time, the water stayed outside my ear, just as it had before the infection.

I fleetingly wondered if I had just received one of the dolphins' notorious healings, but this was a stretch for someone like myself, who at that time was invested in the strength of my own rational mind. Yet, the correction to my ear has held for fifteen years. Moreover, as I have gotten to know the dolphins better during this period and have experienced even more of their healing magic and other powers, I have grown to trust that the healing of my ear was, in fact, my first gift from the dolphins.

The dolphins seem to live continuously in a high-heart state and generously share their healing powers with people as they did with me. As a result, anytime we have brought a friend or child with some medical or emotional challenge to the bay, they have paid particular attention to them. Not only do the dolphins approach the afflicted people soon after they enter the water, but they often point their melons, or the rounded area on the tops of their heads involved with their sonar mechanism, directly at them. Following these encounters, our friends usually feel initially toxic and then considerably better, if not completely well. One woman with fibromyalgia on a Big Island boat trip I took with my girlfriend actually vomited soon after getting into the water with the dolphins. But shortly thereafter, she felt fine and continued to swim with them. To her surprise, she was pain-free and did not need her medications for the remainder of the trip.

Many experience an increased need to urinate following a swim with the dolphins, which may be due to a release of toxins. Others are overwhelmed by a need to sleep. I have also learned to recognize a change in the energy in the bay when the dolphins are flooding it with their healing sonar. Some people like myself are overpowered by the energy and may develop cramps as the dolphins get close to them. I have also noticed my body sometimes vibrating in a gentle manner that feels like purring following time with the dolphins, and this has been reported by others as well. After these healing baths, most tell of feeling both physically and emotionally clearer, healthier, and happier.

Yet, in spite of these results, the source of the dolphins' healing and mood-elevating abilities remains a mystery. I have always felt that it comes from their ability to project their energy, much like a remote control projects its energy to a television set. Then one day this seemed to be confirmed. After noticing a deep gash on Maka's chin, I put my hands up in hopes that I could send enough loving and caring energy to help him heal it. As I did this, I began to wonder if this was how the dolphins do their healing, and I considered taking a class in pranic healing or reiki to learn more about the art of projecting one's energy. While I pondered this idea, Maka slipped underwater and seemed to shoot a surge of energy against the rocks on the other side of the lagoon. This caused a foot of water from the still lagoon to snap loudly against the rocks and send the fish flying. I had witnessed these apparent surges of energy before and assumed they came from the dolphins. But this time, I had the distinct feeling that Maka was showing me how dolphins send their healing energy to others at a time I was pondering the question.

Whatever the source, the dolphins' energies influence ours and entrain us to their more balanced state of harmony, health, and joy. This infusing of our energy with theirs affects not only our emotions and physiology but also our hearts. The value of this is obvious. Yet, it is also supported by the work of Dr. Herbert Benson (*Timeless Healing*, 1996), Gary Zukav (*The Seat of the Soul*, 1989), Caroline Myss (*Anatomy of the Spirit*, 1996), and others, who suggest that our ability to become pervasively loving may have the capacity to elevate and alter our molecular structure and DNA to significantly higher levels. This elevation of our energies is clearly in service of harmony.

the harmony of partnership with humans

When I first met Terry Pinney (*Angels of the Sea*, 1996), she said that even before she swam with dolphins during a visit to a marine park, she felt an urge to press her head against the Plexiglas of a dolphin tank. After doing this, she noticed a vibrational sensation move through her head, neck, and shoulders, and found when she opened her eyes that a dolphin was pressing his head against the partition from the other side. Following that experience, Terry felt she had been opened psychically, and added that she had even been invited by her local police to help locate missing people. She also told me that Iwa and Maka worked with her to help the people she brought to them with healing challenges. Although I was a student of metaphysics and understood such possibilities, I was nonetheless a skeptic and questioned the skills Terry claimed the dolphins had opened in her.

Then one day, when I was watching the dolphin show at the hotel, Terry arrived on the scene. Iwa got very excited when she saw her and behaved more exuberantly than I had ever seen. Terry felt no qualms about loudly imitating a dolphin chirp to communicate with Iwa, and Iwa responded in kind. Then, as the show continued, Iwa kept her eyes riveted on Terry and added several jumps to her routine as Terry squealed and clapped. Even the trainer was surprised by Iwa's exuberance and extra tricks. Following the show, Iwa swam quickly over to Terry and delighted in her greeting. She then began to point her melon at the people Terry had brought for healing, and I felt myself being won over to Terry's claims of psychic connection and healing partnership with the dolphins.

But the story in those early days that most helped me to reverse my skepticism of the dolphins' special powers was that of a beautiful, well-educated, and delightful eleven-year-old with family in both Hawaii and Japan. Kaori could play "Chopsticks" and some very basic tunes on the piano with one hand, but little else. Then one day after swimming with the dolphins, she emerged from the water feeling very light and cleansed and had the sensation that she could fly. That afternoon, she sat down at her grandmother's piano and was able to play a hauntingly beautiful composition with both hands. Kaori felt this gift had come through her from the dolphins, and it is a talent she has retained. As a result, Kaori has produced several tapes and CDs filled with lovely piano pieces that sound uniquely dolphin-like, match the tempo of their swimming, and have been credited for a number of healings, including the full recovery of a dying dog. I had the privilege of hearing this lovely girl play some of her pieces on a grand piano, which had been placed in a movie set on the beach overlooking the dolphins' bay, as the sun set dramatically over the horizon.

the harmony of music

Researchers have found that wild dolphins and their whale cousins are drawn to recorded music played through hydro-phones into the water and are even more interested in live music. They appear to particularly like sounds with high tones such as those produced by flutes and bells, and I have never been on a boat when dolphins and whales failed to show up anytime there was live music aboard.

I first realized the importance of sound and music to dolphins when I began to audibly "coo" into my snorkel as a group of mother and baby dolphins swam beneath me in one of my earlier encounters. My gesture was reinforced by one of the babies wiggling like a happy, floppy puppy as he looked up at me sweetly in response to my cooing. My awareness of this baby's pleasure with my sounds was further supported by my observation of dolphins turning off the course they were traveling on in order to greet me during times I was singing or toning the sound of "om" or "God" into the water through my snorkel.

One day, a young man arrived on the beach with a large bongo drum. An excellent drummer, he began to beat out a compelling rhythm. In no time, the dolphins appeared on the horizon and began from miles out to acknowledge the music by jumping and dancing their way toward shore. As the dolphins drew closer, the drummer beat louder and faster, while the humans found various ways to blend with the rhythm. Before long, the dolphins arrived and began to leap and spin their way in and out among the gleeful swimmers. The drummer kept drumming and the dolphins and people kept dancing as our hearts were rhythmically drawn into the harmony of our shared laughter and joy.

Later, while on the Big Island with my son and daughter-in-law, I took a bongo drum and chime aboard our boat, which we played throughout most of our ride. We soon attracted about seventy pilot whales who accompanied us for close to an hour, obviously enjoying our music. When we later stopped to drop our hydrophones into the water, I could hear a humpback whale mimicking the tones from my chime, so I responded in kind, and we played back and forth to each other for a while. Whenever I made two or three tones, he would follow my lead, and when I returned to one tone, so did he. Later, we attracted about fifty dolphins who accompanied our boat for another hour also enjoying our drumming while swimming alongside us closer than I had previously witnessed.

Although I was not surprised by the cetacean response to music in the open ocean, it caught me off guard to see how engrossed the hotel dolphins, Keola and Kama, became when I got the idea to sing "O Holy Night" to them one day. As I sang, both seemed to listen intently. Then, when I finished, Keola blew three large bubbles in a row, something I had never seen him do. I was beginning to realize that dolphins communicate with symbolic language and wondered if he thought my singing was a three-bubble performance.

On another day, when I toned "om" to these captive dolphins, Keola again responded with the most interest by making similar sounds and clearly trying to accompany me. When I switched to "He's Got the Whole World in His Hands," Keola joined me note for note for a few bars of the song, although his imitation of me was still not exact. Kama remained in the area listening to us and joined in for a few clumsily produced notes, then in response to my smiles of encouragement, he opened his mouth and showed his teeth in a mock smile. I got the feeling he was diverting attention from his musical skills, which were lesser than those of Keola. I later read of studies conducted at the Dolphin Institute in Hawaii, showing that dolphins could not only recognize melodies but were able to imitate the sounds as well as the gestures of humans. Thus, I discovered that my hunch about being imitated in song and gesture by these dolphins was supported by research.

interspecies harmony

In addition to harmony in their environments, among themselves, and in music, dolphins enjoy harmony with other species. Thus, not only are they kind to humans, but they also extend kindness to other species. For example, they are known to assist killer whales giving birth and have been observed playing with other sea life as well as dogs brought to them by boat. One dolphin aficionado reports going to Queensland to meet with some dolphins there. Thinking his Rottweiler might pose a problem for the dolphins, he locked the unhappy fellow in the car for the first three days of his trip. The dolphins didn't show until the fourth day, when he allowed the dog to join him, at which time they befriended the Rottweiler first and then made friends with his owner.

My favorite image of interspecies harmony among dolphins and whales comes from the joy they find in each other. Whenever I have been on boats throughout the world in search of cetaceans, we have often encountered them playing together. One friend was graced with seeing an enormous whale gliding beneath her with five or six dolphins hitching a ride on the whale's outstretched pectorals.

harmony with nature and others

The environments the dolphins and whales select for their nurseries and winter playgrounds are the most beautiful in the world. They are composed of indigo and turquoise ocean coves and bays stocked with an abundance of living corals, colorful fish, turtles, and rays beneath the sea, while sunshine, sea birds, and butterflies fill the air above. These coves and bays are also characterized by harmonious communities of wildlife or people living on the land that encircles them. Whenever disharmony erupts in these villages, the dolphins and whales are known to move on to a new site, at least for the duration of the disruption.

I first noticed this during a summer when our dolphin-loving community became very connected, followed by a period when our harmony was broken. Although we were a divergent group, representing both city and country, rich and poor, highly educated and unschooled, metaphysicians and scientists, we had bonded around our love for the dolphins. We shared food, laughter, stories, music, and our hearts. During the period when we were close, the dolphins spent all day dancing along the surface of our bay, playing with us for up to three or four hours at a time. It was a wonderfully happy period for all of us. That was the summer of 1995.

Then the gossip began, and our group slowly divided into a number of conflicting factions. The dolphins didn't show up when conflict broke out but rewarded us with their presence whenever we tried to solve our problems. In addition to the dissension amongst ourselves, negative energies were gathering in our relationships with the dolphins. People were developing commercial enterprises which attracted large numbers of visitors to swim with the dolphins without providing adequate information about how to interact with them. As a result, a new trend of chasing every dolphin who came up for air replaced the one we had originally established of letting the dolphins come to us and lead the way in our interactions. As the numbers and chasing increased, the energies at the bay were completely altered. What had once been a joyful dance between species turned into a competitive endeavor with swarms of people chasing after the dolphins and cutting in front of others to get the "best" experience. The needs of the dolphins were completely overlooked during this period, and harassment took the place of harmony.

In spite of the dedication to harmony the dolphins had revealed in the structuring of their own community, as well as in their interactions with us, their peace was now being overrun by our self-serving ways. Thus, rather than remain with us for extended periods of dancing and playing, the hunted dolphins could no longer stay. Our human-dolphin interactions had been converted to ones in which people were coming to the beautiful home of these high-level beings and chasing them around their own dwelling. The foolishness of this approach called to mind an image of people running through the forest after deer in an effort to befriend them. Yet it was even more parallel to chasing an enlightened master around his temple in hopes of sharing his light. Self-interest had caused people to let go of the most basic form of common sense and courtesy, and the rules of our world had supplanted the harmonious ones of the dolphins.

At first, the dolphins handled our insensitivity to their needs by attempting to give everyone a brief visit before leaving the area. Yet even the dolphins' saintly response to the rudeness of the people swarming their bay failed to raise the level of human consciousness. The people remained relentless in their pursuit of the dolphins and openly competed with each other over the now brief encounters with them. In fact, they accelerated their chasing behaviors and swam farther and faster after them, kicking each other in the process. Numerous kayaks were launched in order to track down the escaping dolphins, followed by larger boats, some of which ran directly into the dolphins' pod at full speed. The area soon became a sad reflection of human insensitivity and greed.

Over time, the divisions between the people on the beach also deepened, and the dolphins made themselves increasingly scarce. Then, a drowning that seemed to be a result of this new attitude of competitiveness further clouded our clarity and hearts. Seemingly affected more by our unkindness to each other than to them, the dolphins abruptly stopped coming to the bay altogether for a period of time.

But dolphins don't make judgments or hold grudges, and it wasn't too many months before they returned on an abbreviated basis, particularly on the days when we asked for forgiveness and behaved lovingly toward them and each other. Although many of the people on the beach continued their rift, chased the dolphins, and polluted the bay, the dolphins offered us periodic visits and fleeting encounters of play. Yet, because these were now sporadic and brief, most of the commercial operations didn't survive, and people who wanted guarantees of an experience stopped coming.

This was the dolphins' gentle answer to the quarreling and rudeness of people. While remaining as loving and tolerant as possible, they were eventually forced to change the form of their generous gift of abundant joy until humans could learn to respond with improved manners and grace. Their visits became less frequent and lasted only briefly.

After a year or so, we were given a new chance. Because the crowds had thinned and manners were mildly improved, dolphin-initiated encounters gradually resumed. We were given a new opportunity to enjoy occasional days reminiscent of the kinds of encounters we had experienced fifteen years ago. Yet people persisted in chasing and quarreling among themselves, and the joy of the early days never fully returned. And so—with love in my heart as the dolphins have taught me to maintain—I gently caution people to mind their manners if they want to continue to receive the dolphins' gifts of friendship, harmony, and joy, as well as the wondrous lessons they are coming to our shores to teach us. (For information on how to approach cetaceans, see "Guidelines for Successful Cetacean Encounters" on page xiv.)

After about a year of enjoying renewed, although altered, connections with our cetacean friends, the U.S. Navy conducted sonar tests in the spring of 1998, in which they directed high levels of sonar directly at whales in Hawaiian waters to see how they would react. While civilian researchers and private citizens observed unusual behavior and several deaths during this period, the navy failed to investigate these concerns and denied any problems. Although the sonar was later proved to be lethal for cetaceans and was legally stopped, it is now back in the water in full force and with less restraint, due to military exemptions.

I realized while recording the dolphins' first three gifts of kindness, joy, and harmony how quickly humans gloss over the profundity of these qualities rather than viewing them as the critical components to the happiness they truly represent. I also wondered if our minimizing the importance of these powerful personality traits of the higher self is the reason humanity has not succeeded in developing as much kindness, harmony, and joy as the dolphins have attained.

the harmony of blended hearts
creates a loving and joyful
world. the reverse is also true.

CHAPTER 7

the fourth gift:
exalted intelligence used wisely

Great scientists are not afraid of new frontiers.
—Margaret Mead

Each of the dolphins' gifts of character as revealed to me not only built on the gift before it, but also exposed an ever-evolving tapestry of the nature of dolphins. The fourth of these is the gift of exalted intelligence used wisely.

It is interesting to note that, although humans claim to highly value the gift of intelligence, we consistently fail to nurture this quality in our children or inspire it in our species. This is most profoundly reflected in our crumbling educational system, all too often known for its abundance of spirit-killing homework, while lacking vital attention to the development of our children's thinking skills or genuine wisdom. Moreover, when confronted with genius in others, we deny and dispute it, and many sages in our midst have suffered our misunderstanding and ridicule. In view of this, as we investigate the nature of intelligence in dolphins, it will be helpful to stay open to all possibilities presented, as well as to search for ways to support this quality in our own species and others.

from simple to sublime

Once, while sailing in the Bahamas with friends, we came across three captive dolphins swimming in their sea-pen. They were the property of the owner of the *Flipper* dolphins, who had all been moved to Cuba except for these three; they had been left behind until the nursing baby was old enough to travel. We befriended the caretaker who watched over the dolphins, and he allowed us to enter the ocean pen and swim with them for as long as we wished.

The large bottle-nosed dolphins approached me in unison the moment I entered the water, peered into my eyes as they cut several swaths around me, and then swam off to the corner of their pen. Within minutes they were back, swimming directly at me in a fast and frightening manner before they turned away just in time to avoid a collision. When I made squealing dolphin sounds, their circling accelerated, and they began to dart excitedly in and out between my friend and myself, stopping abruptly to reverse positions and circle us some more. They seemed overly rambunctious, and because I didn't know them or their histories, I wasn't sure they wouldn't hurt us, so I stopped chirping and quieted my energies, hoping they would follow my lead. Fortunately, they did.

Once they calmed down, their favorite game appeared to be one in which a dolphin would circle me slowly while holding a fixed gaze between his eye and mine. As I turned in a circle to maintain eye contact, he gradually increased his speed, forcing me to go faster to stay in the game. He would then accelerate his speed so that, even though I was at the hub of the circle, I couldn't keep up and was forced to drop out. The dolphin would then prance away swishing his tail and vocalizing victoriously before beginning the game again.

Next, he got very close to me and seemed to want me to touch him. Although I had never previously sensed such an invitation, nor had I ever reached to touch a dolphin before, I felt such a strong call to do so in this situation that I slowly extended my hand. The moment I did, the dolphin backed his body away to a position within an inch from my outstretched fingers and maintained this exact distance as he rapidly circled me. Again, I couldn't keep up and was forced to drop out, which sent him off clucking to his corner again.

When it was time to leave, I sensed the dolphins didn't want us to go, and I could feel the loneliness of their isolation. Following this thought, the mother swam very close to me as her baby nursed, which I took as a sign that she had felt my caring and was acknowledging me with this show of trust.

After saying my good-byes, I was surprised to find myself struggling to get out of the water onto the platform, as my ex-husband pushed from the water and my friend pulled from the platform. The longer it took, the harder we laughed, until I fell back into the water weak from hilarity, only to find one of the dolphins standing in an upright position beneath the surface watching me. When I looked at him our eyes met, and he shook his head from side to side about four times. I burst out laughing underwater, and he resumed shaking his head as I now choked on my laughter, not wanting to miss a moment of his look of humored disdain. Once we finally got me out of the water and piled into our boat to leave, all three dolphins swam along the edge of their pen and kept us in sight for as long as they could. The attendant had shared that wild dolphins come alongside the pen from time to time to visit with the captives, and I hoped they would come soon to ease the loneliness I sensed in them.

Although these dolphins were able to reveal more of their intelligence than most captives because of their freedom to initiate activities and respond appropriately, they still seemed younger than the dolphins I had met in the wild. As a result, this experience underscored the common concern about our basing so much dolphin research on this population of captives taken from their families while still very young or born in captivity to those who were caught before they themselves had matured.

In contrast to the simple and playful sweetness of these confined dolphins, the following story about two wild orcas, the most dominant of all the cetaceans, demonstrates the highly sentient, aware, and intelligent nature of this species when found in their own natural habitat. In this instance, as two loggers were working from a hillside in British Columbia, one of them deliberately let go of a log in order to maliciously hit a pod of orcas passing below. One of the whales was hit in the back hard enough to injure but not kill him. The whales initially moved on, but they returned later that night just in time to meet up with the loggers' boat and tip it over as the two men rowed back to camp. The man who hit the whale with the log was never seen again, while the other man was not touched and survived to tell the story.

I have encountered equally aware and intelligent behaviors in wild dolphins, as well as in some captives who are able to discern the attitudes and essences of others. For example, one day when my ex-husband and I were in the bay together, a small group of dolphins had turned off course to bound excitedly toward us. As they were coming, we started to quarrel. The dolphins lifted their faces out of the water in unison, paused to stare at us in disbelief, and then made a U-turn and left for the day.

In contrast, when dolphins discern positive energy in a person they often initiate some sort of interaction with them. When they feel particularly close, they may even stand upright before them. For instance, after a long separation from each other, Donald, the bottle-nosed ambassador who had befriended Dr. Horace Dobbs, stood upright before him for about thirty seconds when they first reconnected.

This honoring gesture has been observed in captive dolphins as well. A dramatic example of it occurred when an entire petting pool full of dolphins at a Florida dolphinarium stood upright in front of a group of singers serenading them in harmony, a behavior dolphins particularly enjoy. Another happened when a woman involved in the Texas Marine Mammal rescue program later went to another city where Mattie, one of her favorite survivors, had been placed several months before. When she arrived, Mattie greeted her from this upright position, while engaging her in prolonged eye contact. As mentioned earlier, I was given this same rare greeting by Iwa and her offspring on several occasions, as well as by a wild dolphin in Bimini and by Hawaii's Sea Life Park dolphins, Laukani, Laka, and Nehoa.

This action looks and feels very intimate and respectful, much like someone bowing to acknowledge the person being greeted while saying, "Namaste," or "the God in me recognizes the God in you." It feels as though the dolphins recognize you not only physically but also energetically and are expressing their appreciation of those who connect with them deeply through the heart. Even though this degree of discernment of character and quality of response indicates a high level of awareness, humans have been slow to fully acknowledge or measure this sentient nature or discerning intelligence in dolphins.

some barriers to assessing dolphin intelligence

Most scientists operate on the assumption that humans are superior to all others and vigorously defend this position rather than remaining open to discovering higher levels of intelligence in other species. Unfortunately, this limiting view prevents them from seeing intelligent behaviors, even when they are clearly presented. For example, in a newspaper article discussing a dolphin funeral procession observed along the California coastline, one scientist assumed the dolphins did not realize that the dolphin they were carrying was dead.

To support the assumption that only humans possess a higher level of intelligence, many scientists invoke the concept of anthropomorphism, or the projection of "human qualities" onto "animals." They hold that all behavior that might be interpreted as "intelligent," "aware," or "conscious" must be human or anthropomorphic in nature and that seeing these qualities in other species is a result of a naive and erroneous projection of human qualities onto them. Such scientists' bias relegates all behaviors exercised by other members of the animal kingdom to the category of food-gathering, mating, migratory patterns, curiosity, or defense.

In fact, this position motivated American naturalists to suggest changing the adjective "friendly," selected by Mexican boatmen to describe the gray whales who approach their boats, to "curious." With such a suggestion, American scientists remove any possibility of interpreting this loving cetacean gesture of friendship as anything conscious or purposeful and consign it instead to the category of simple "animalistic" curiosity.

The irony of this position is that most people who have had an opportunity for extended contact, even if only with captive cetaceans, suspect that these large-brained, highly intelligent mammals may possess even greater intelligence and wisdom than humans, and many view the friendship cetaceans extend to humanity as their effort to raise our level of consciousness.

Yet, we remain stubbornly reluctant to seriously probe this possibility. Instead, we stick to studies of mechanistic science in which only those things that can be perceived by our five senses and then measured and replicated under controlled conditions are viewed as valid. As a result of this narrow focus on the limited world of physical markings, migratory patterns, food-gathering, and mating behaviors, the more exciting but non-material mysteries of intention, healing, and telepathy are ridiculed rather than studied.

The limitation of this arrangement was underscored for me at the bay one day, four years into my experiences with the dolphins, when a team of scientists arrived at the bay to begin a dolphin study. Their research was designed to determine dolphins' migratory patterns, to measure the impact swimmers had on them, and to get acquainted. The scientists were individually delightful people and the goals of their study uniquely progressive and interesting. Yet, some of them assumed that because they were scientists, they knew more than others who had been swimming with the dolphins for a number of years. Some of them viewed only their science-based observations and experiences as valid, and they remained markedly uninterested in the observations of others. I found this especially interesting since many of the swimmers who were not part of the science team possessed higher degrees, in a variety of fields, than those on the team.

On this particular day, I entered the water about fifty yards from one of these scientists at a time when no dolphins were in the bay. My goal was to test my new discovery that I could attract the dolphins to me by focusing my intention on them while sending vocal tones and heart-based energies into the water to draw them to me. After succeeding within the next fifteen minutes in attracting a group of about thirty dolphins, who were now surrounding me, this young scientist swam over to my area, getting between me and the dolphins as she rushed toward them at a perpendicular angle.

Because she had moved quickly and directly toward the dolphins—a behavior that more experienced swimmers knew would chase them away—the dolphins turned and headed back out to sea. The scientist began hurriedly to record the identifying markings of the departing dolphins on her underwater notepad and seemed to consider the encounter a success. Yet, not only had she failed to take notice of me or the connection between me and the dolphins, she was also unaware of having chased the dolphins away. This demonstrated for me why we need to listen to the views of everyone, including the scientists, but must not allow any one group's perceptions to hold us to a narrow range of vision. By opening up the field, we not only free scientists to look at more possibilities without fear of ridicule, but gain a broader understanding ourselves by including everyone's perceptions.

The final barriers to our awareness of the sentient, cognizant, and wise nature of dolphin intelligence comes from a sweet but narrow view perpetuated by most marine parks. Because the majority of park dolphins are caught very young for the sole purpose of performance, they are usually viewed as simple, circus-like performers. Moreover, because of the parks' entertainment goals, dolphin trainers rely principally on basic operant conditioning. Thus, rather than sincerely probing the intelligence of this group of dolphins, most park trainers view them as actors and spend their time conditioning them to obey and perform for their shows. Their subsequently shallow view of the dolphins as "cute" is passed onto the public in parks' "educational" programs.

Yet, in spite of so few efforts to probe the intelligence of captive dolphins, the studies that have been conducted readily demonstrate that they not only learn quickly and possess extraordinary intelligence, communication skills, insight, and imagination, but are also clearly able to problem-solve rather than using trial and error to gain correct answers.

In fact, their abilities have attracted the attention of the U.S. Navy, whose captive dolphins have been reported to be trusted enough to transport military hardware and serve as mine sweepers and possibly more, according to rumor. In addition, the navy has conducted most of the research done on dolphins, which is also reported to be relegated primarily to classified information.

One story that escaped naval secrecy was told to me by a civilian who helped the military train their dolphins. It seems the navy had long conceded that dolphin sonar was more sophisticated than the navy's most advanced technology. Thus, in order to improve their own equipment, they were running a number of tests to glean additional insights as to how the dolphins' sonar works. During one of these exercises two dolphins were asked to identify an object. Then as the dolphins proceeded to perform the task, the researchers flooded their sonar from behind in order to scramble it enough to interfere with their ability to read the image. The dolphins resolved this problem by quickly arranging between them to have one send his signal upward to read the top half of the image while the other sent his down to pick up the bottom half. Then they put their pictures together and correctly identified the image.

When the navy began its turn to identify the same object, the dolphins turned in tandem to face the naval equipment and proceeded to flood it with enough sonar of their own to disable it in kind. This story not only reveals the high level of awareness the dolphins possess but the wry humor that goes with a wise use of intelligence.

what we've learned from research

Even though most dolphin research is based on studies of captive dolphins handicapped by the stresses of capture and confinement, as well as their lack of opportunity to have learned from their mothers and communities, results are promising. For example, French researcher Dr. Javis Bastian found that two dolphins, Doris and Buzz, were able to conduct abstract communication through a soundproofed wall separating them in order to devise a plan that would enable them to succeed in completing a complex task.

The University of Hawaii's Dolphin Institute, directed by Lou Herman, discovered that dolphins have excellent short- and long-term memory for things both seen and heard, can interpret television images without any training, and have easily learned and demonstrate a keen interest in the grammar of the sign and auditory languages they are being taught and readily understand. They have also noted that dolphins are not only able to mimic on command but can also determine that if a human lifts a leg, lifting a tail fluke will provide the best comparable body part. And in order to accommodate a command to go under an object, they lift the object from the floor of their tank.

The Project Delphis study conducted at Sea Life Park's Earthtrust under the guidance of Dr. Ken Marten recently concluded that dolphins possess the awareness that television is a representation of reality, that they are self-aware, that they understand that mirrors represent images of themselves (something that cannot be taught and must be intuited), and that they are able to communicate with each other when separated by correctly figuring out and using a two-way phone and one-way video linkup supplied by the experimenters.

What is surprising is that it has taken science so long to conduct the kinds of studies that expose this level of dolphin intelligence. Although we are slow to admit it, these results force us to concede the truth of the claims of trainers and others suggesting that dolphins, at the very least, share the unique category of intelligence we previously believed only humans possessed.

what we've learned from observation

Interestingly, scientists conducting research frequently find their most dramatic discoveries about dolphin intelligence in the behaviors the dolphins voluntarily demonstrate outside the structure of the research protocols.

For example, Tuffy, a dolphin working with the Sealab II capsule project, was being trained to rescue divers pretending to be in trouble. Once, when Tuffy successfully performed a simulated rescue, the rescued diver couldn't get his bag of fish open, so rather than reward Tuffy for his rescue, he waved him away. But Tuffy did not move. Instead he stared at the man in disbelief for a moment before raising his flipper and gently bopping him over the head. This same dolphin later realized that one of the divers was in real trouble and needed genuine rescue, so he responded quickly and went to his aid.

In another case, a dolphin being trained to assassinate was observed refusing to attack his target and resting his chin on the man's shoulder instead. Another dolphin was receiving his reward for correct responses from a feeding machine containing fish that had spoiled. To bring this problem to his trainer's attention, the dolphin began to give all incorrect responses until his trainer figured out that something was wrong, investigated the problem, and remedied the situation.

Another newly captured dolphin demonstrated his understanding of an error in his training program when the trainer failed to reward him for doing a behavior correctly. He responded to her mistake by rushing around the tank, then breaching, and finally going to the far side of the tank where he turned his back on the trainer. It took an apology to lure this dolphin back to the session, but when it was over, he approached his trainer to stroke her arm with his flipper as if to let her know it was OK.

In other cases, dolphins will interject just enough play and teasing outside the parameters of their training session or research study that they think their trainer will tolerate. In fact, the more tolerant the trainer is, the more these dolphins will push their boundaries in order to reveal more of their own personalities and abilities. For example, because my hotel dolphin friend Nehoa was allowed by her trainer to carry hats under her fins, she used the hats to amuse hotel visitors as well as herself. Eventually, Maka added the hats to his repertoire of comedy, but rather than strut with them as Nehoa did, he used them as props to imitate humans.

When the easygoing trainer left and was replaced by a series of less tolerant ones, the hats were removed and this delightful aspect of the dolphins' personalities could no longer be seen.

When trainers get emotionally involved with the dolphins and believe in their abilities, the dolphins respond with even more interactive, playful, and innovative behaviors. In fact, it is these original behaviors that catch the attention of a trainer who then rewards the behavior and incorporates it into the inventory of tricks the rest of the dolphins are taught.

It is interesting to note that dolphins don't do well with research protocols that require replication and, as anyone who has had direct experience or trained them will tell you, they simply don't like duplication. In fact they seem to get bored and feel controlled by being asked to repeat responses over and over and often resist conforming to this human need for repetition, sometimes even when it means going without food rewards.

When this quality in dolphins was first noted, Karen Pryor designed a study in which dolphins were asked to perform original behaviors of their own design rather than repeat those already learned. Her first subject, a female, particularly enjoyed this activity and produced many new behaviors once she realized she was being rewarded for originality. However, when the next dolphin asked to do original behaviors took longer to figure out the goal, the test was deemed invalid simply because the same promising results were not easily attained by the second dolphin. This lack of replication needed to fulfill scientific protocol and the pessimistic conclusions that were drawn about dolphin abilities, owing to the second dolphin's slowness to understand the task, brought this kind of testing to a halt and set dolphin studies back for years.

Fortunately, years later the Dolphin Institute followed up this study with an improved design and found that all of their dolphins were able to learn the concept and produce original behaviors. They further taught their dolphins a sign that means "create your own behavior" as well as one that says "do it in tandem." Whenever these signs are coupled, two dolphins are consistently able to simultaneously perform the same original behavior, although the researchers don't yet know how they do it. People who have interacted with dolphins outside the limited parameters of research protocols attribute this ability to a combination of telepathic skills coupled with a high level of dolphin intelligence that our researchers have only begun to uncover.

dolphin intelligence used wisely

When we assume intelligence in dolphins until proven otherwise, rather than the reverse, we are free to recognize how fully sentient and intelligent they are. From this new perspective, we can observe their behaviors with a broader openness to what they mean and, thus, see new possibilities we previously discounted. If we also understand, as Joseph Chilton Pearce ("Waking Up to the Holographic Heart," *Wild Duck Review,* by Casey Walker) and others teach, that the wisdom that reaches beyond intelligence can be accessed only through the heart, it becomes clear that dolphin wisdom is inspired by the heart-based higher-self qualities they so consistently express. If we then look for a combination of intelligence and wisdom in dolphins rather than fight against these possibilities, we might be surprised by what we find.

new discoveries that suggest a greater intelligence and deeper wisdom

In 1991, the captive dolphins at Sea Life Park initiated blowing bubbles while watching themselves in the mirror and then played with their bubbles in a variety of ways such as diving through the various structures they created with them. Around this same time, a whale cousin in Boston Harbor began to blow giant cloud bubbles and cigar rings, which he liked to pop his head through to the delight of his daily audiences. Amazon River dolphins were simultaneously seen emitting air from their mouths to form necklaces of bubbles, which they would then pass through or bite. During this same time, a number of other wild and captive dolphins and whales were observed throughout the world blowing bubbles in all sizes and shapes. I have been privileged to see many of these wonderful bubbles blown by both dolphins and whales in the open ocean as well as in captivity.

The concurrent appearance of these bubbles in so many places, similar to the simultaneous occurrence of increased cetacean visits with humans all over the world during this same period, begs the question of how and why these activities are appearing in simultaneous clusters. One theory explained in the work of Larry Dossey (*Recovering the Soul,* 1989) and others is that it occurs thanks to a shared awareness among cetaceans.

Dr. Ken Marten, director of Project Delphis at Hawaii's Earthtrust, and his staff had the good fortune to closely study some of these bubbles when blown by the Sea Life Park dolphins on the other side of their observation window at the park's research site. He describes this phenomenon as something that would amaze a physicist and has published his team's groundbreaking observations in the August 1996 *Scientific American.*

The various bubbles blown by these dolphins from their mouths or blowholes are not like typical bubbles that break up in the water but appear as smooth and stable rings of air, silver bubbles, or a series of tiny bubbles that linger in the water. The stability of these bubbles appears to be a result of the dolphins using their sonar to control and stabilize them in some way. Once the bubbles are formed, the dolphins play with them by swimming through them, biting at them, sucking them into their mouths, playing volleyball with them, or collapsing them into a cluster of smaller silver bubbles. Or the dolphins might rearrange the shape of a ring bubble by turning it over on itself to create the sign of infinity, merge it with another bubble, or turn it into a longer ring or corkscrew.

Forming a bubble ring takes greater skill, since the dolphins must first create a swirling spherical vortex in the water by using their dorsal fins or turning their tail flukes vertically in the water and snapping them as they turn to generate a swirl. Next they use sonar clicks to locate the vortex and inject bubbles from their blowholes or mouths into it, creating a swirling ring one to two feet long. Interestingly, these swirling rings are the same design as torus bubbles, which are a structure included in the new string and unified field theories of the universe.

The bubble phenomenon was first noticed at Sea Life Park when two babies who were alone in a tank began to create their first bubbles. One of these babies was Tinkerbell, daughter of the dominant female Laka. Tinkerbell later showed a particular interest in sharing her bubbles with her trainer and demonstrated her ability to also form more complex helices. She does this by first blowing some bubbles and then using her dorsal fin to gather the bubbles together and coil them into a spiraling helix as long as ten to fifteen feet.

Not only are these helices more challenging to create, they are especially interesting in view of the fact that the wild dolphins have often acted out the spiraling helix spin by twirling their bodies into this pattern in front of me. They begin by gathering three to six or more dolphins together, and on some invisible cue they dive downward and begin spinning and weaving in and out between each other, looking like strands as they weave themselves into a spinning braid that looks like a DNA helix pattern as it appears under a microscope. Next, the dolphins turn upward while continuing to spin together and accelerate their speed as they unbraid themselves in an explosion of energy. This is interesting in view of new questions and conversations among scientists regarding the prospect of DNA's serving as antennae in search of new possibilities. This in turn raises a chicken-and-egg question about the role of DNA as the selector of our patterns or reflector of the ones we have chosen—or both.

By engaging in these bubble-blowing and spinning activities, are the dolphins trying to tell us something meaningful with the use of symbolic language and metaphor? In the event this is true, what might they be saying and why? At the very least, they have demonstrated that even their children understand fluid dynamics and the physics of vortexes and helices at a level well beyond the comprehension of most people and well enough to produce them. This alone is profound and something we cannot ignore. But what else are they trying to show us? What message besides their own level of awareness and intelligence are they trying to convey?

At the very least, the dolphins are clearly reflecting some mesmerizing, powerful, and holographic pattern in nature. Is their repeated demonstration of this pattern accidental or purposeful? If it is purposeful, as it seems, surely they know more and would like to share their wisdom with us. Yet, in order for them to do so, we must be willing to listen. To begin, we must allow the dolphins to talk to us and then strive to understand. If we would put our superiority on the shelf for long enough to take this step, I suspect we would be delightfully surprised by what we could learn. But until the day we decide to do that, the dolphins will continue as they always have to talk to us in a number of surprising and delightful ways.

For example, well before the first edition of this book was published, my first husband and I had decided to end our marriage. Several years later, while dating my current husband, Dr. Tom Merrill, it was apparent to me early on that he is both bright and logical as well as data-based in his approach to understanding things. Although I am also logical and like to ground my intuitive discoveries in science, I was not sure he would be comfortable with the extent of my sentient and intuitive nature. Thus, although I was very attracted to him, I was also clear that I did not want to spend my remaining years with someone who was uncomfortable with this part of me. And so I made a point of revealing all of the many surreal experiences I had enjoyed with the dolphins. One of the most phenomenal of these was going into the water on days the dolphins were in the bay and noticing stacks of miniature torus bubbles piled on the tops of my fingernails, where they remained for about thirty seconds before being released one at a time. I could see by the look on his face that I might have gone too far with this story, but it was the same look everyone else gave me—and the same look I would have given someone sharing a similar story with me—so I didn't hold it against him.

Then, to my surprise, on our first day of connecting together with dolphins, as soon as we dove into the water, a stack of these bubbles appeared on each of his fingernails. The expression on his face was priceless. He is a gold-medal-winning canoe paddler who has swum in Hawaiian waters all of his life, yet had never seen anything like this. He tested and retested this reality a couple of times while the dolphins kept the bubbles coming—but it didn't take long before he was convinced. He then looked up at me and grinned as he pointed with delight at his bubbles. By giving this reality-based data lover his own experience of this phenomenon, the dolphins had found a swift and playful way to add credibility to my claims.

opening the way to two-way conversations

Unfortunately, most cetacean research still requires that dolphins respond only to commands to perform tricks or other simple tasks and does not seek ways to let them talk to us. Even a group of Hawaii-based researchers who have developed progressive sign and auditory languages the dolphins are easily able to learn have not yet found a way to allow the dolphins to talk back. Yet, in spite of our lack of interest in letting the dolphins tell us what they know, some dolphins have found a way to break through.

For example, researcher John Lilly was teaching a dolphin named Elvar to mimic a number of words and phrases, which Elvar could execute quite well. Then one day when cosmologist Carl Sagan visited Lilly at his laboratory, Elvar swam up to him and rolled over on his back, indicating he wanted Sagan to rub his stomach. After Sagan obliged him, Elvar swam away and returned to roll over again, this time with his belly about a foot under the water. Sagan now rolled up his sleeves to reach underwater to again rub Elvar's stomach. Showing great excitement, Elvar swam away and returned several more times, going deeper underwater each time. Finally, not wanting to get entirely soaked, Sagan ignored

Elvar, who then responded by standing up on his tail directly in front of Sagan and clearly proclaiming, "More." This not only demonstrated Elvar's understanding of his new words but that he was able to devise a way to reveal his ability to use them in context.

Another way to listen to cetaceans as we probe the depths of their understanding is through our common language of music. In this regard, a dramatic display of cetacean intelligence is revealed in Jim Nollman's enchanting tapes of orca whales joining the jam sessions of his live band. These are not only delightfully touching but startling to the average person listening to them, even though they were rejected by the scientific community because the whales' individual performances could not be consistently replicated. I have heard tapes of the mother and calf most interested in this activity interjecting their own notes at appropriate times into the beat of Nollman's eclectic band, which was playing music to them through hydrophones dropped from his boat. The calf even joined the group by himself following his mother's death and, during this special jam session, assumed the lead note. Was the calf using symbolic language to convey that he was not only interested in participating in the band but was also able to assume the position of musical leader? If the circumstances were reversed, what chance would we have of taking the lead in a whale chorus? Another point of interest is that Nollman telepathically tells the whales what day, time, and where the concerts will be held, and the whales magically show up at the right place on time.

new horizons

Since dolphins have indicated as best they can that they do in fact understand us, it seems appropriate that we try to understand them as well. And because so many trainers and others with long-term exposure to dolphins believe that dolphins are telepathic, this seems like a good place to start. Yet, because our society has rejected the notion of telepathy for so long, our resistance to taking this step is strong. However, in spite of our opposition to uncovering whether or not dolphins engage in telepathic communication, the dolphins' may have already established their ability to use it. Decide for yourself as you read about a study conducted by Scott Jones and Jan Northup on May 6, 1984, with a dolphin named Lucky at SeaArama in Galveston, Texas.

In this study, Scott typed five instructions on separate sheets of paper and placed them in sealed envelopes. Jan, who did not know what instructions had been included in the envelopes, entered the tank area where Lucky was waiting. Two judges without knowledge of what the instructions said were assigned to observe and record all of Lucky's behaviors. Next, a judge rolled a pair of dice to determine which envelope to hand to Jan first. Then Jan opened the designated envelope, read the instructions to herself, and mentally sent Lucky the message she had just read without any hand or other signals.

Lucky was able to successfully perform the first two instructions, but a problem developed when he got to the third. Unknown to Scott when he wrote the instructions, Lucky would not be able to accommodate the instruction to jump in this particular tank since the roof over the top of it was too low for a jump. Thus, rather than attempt the requested jump, Lucky sent a thought to Jan indicating he couldn't make the jump but would do something similar. When Jan received this message telepathically, she looked up and saw that the roof would prevent a jump and understood that Lucky was attempting to replicate a jump when he went to the center of the pool and bobbed up and down. For the fourth instruction, Lucky added a very dolphin-like element of surprise. He performed the task before Jan had a chance to open the envelope or read the instructions. When Jan then opened the envelope, she was startled to find that Lucky had correctly performed according to the instructions, as he also did with the instructions in the fifth and final envelope after Jan opened and read it.

When it came time to rate Lucky's performance, the judges marked his refused jump and the prematurely performed response as incorrect. This not only underscores the difference between our two species but also reveals the kinds of valuable information we miss as a result of our strict adherence to scientific experimental designs. But for anyone not bound by the limits of research protocol, it's clear that Lucky successfully demonstrated his ability to receive instructions telepathically.

Especially interesting, too, is that Lucky was a rescued dolphin rather than one born in captivity or captured in his youth. As such, Lucky had been raised to adulthood by free dolphins and had been exposed to the teachings of both his mother and his elders. As a result, he was uniquely qualified to demonstrate for us the full abilities of dolphins rather than the less-developed ones of so many captive dolphins.

Later studies using soundproofed walls have more easily proved the telepathic skills of cetaceans who respond to requests for behavior sent to them telepathically through these barriers without benefit of any auditory or other clues.

summary

The body of research, combined with my own and others' direct observations, give validity to the fact that dolphins are highly intelligent beings with a complex system of linguistic sounds and sonar-imaging skills, as well as strong evidence that they are telepathic. There is also good support for the idea that they use these abilities to tune into deep concepts outside our awareness from the universal morphogenetic field and have at least some understanding of fluid dynamics and physics. Yet, in spite of these findings, we remain stubbornly unsure as to how intelligent dolphins really are and whether or not they possess language.

Given this backdrop of human reluctance to honor either the intelligence or language of dolphins, I was startled by an unusual communication they would later initiate with me as I sat on the beach of their bay.

the question isn't whether or not
the dolphins can talk but whether or
not we are listening.
once we begin to listen, a wonderful
new world will be revealed.

CHAPTER 8

the fifth gift:
telepathy serving clarity and truth

Clarity can be achieved only by being fully naked before others about who we really are.

The gift of telepathy's serving clarity and truth was revealed to me much in the way a surprise party is presented, and it was this gift that opened my mind to new levels of honesty in all of my relationships.

Swimming with my dolphin friends had become a regular activity for me, and each connection revealed more about the conscious nature of these intelligent beings. After a year of my enjoying this playful friendship, something happened that completely altered my view of dolphins. And with this alteration, my view of the world was changed as well.

I had been sitting on the beach at the bay reading a book when I felt drawn to look through my binoculars at a group of dolphins journeying along the horizon. I watched them swim in a westward direction for a while and then dive in unison and surface a few yards ahead followed by more swimming and another dive. Suddenly, my idle observation of their rhythmic path was interrupted by an unexpected notion that the dolphins would not continue in this direction and that I would need to move my binoculars eastward to pick them up again. This made no sense, but I responded to the idea since it had registered so strongly in my mind.

As I focused my binoculars on an eastward point along the horizon, I was startled when a dolphin jumped into my sights. Following this jump, a second impulse told me to reverse my binoculars and move them about twenty yards to the west. Again I complied with this odd prompting and found another dolphin jumping into my sights. A shiver ran through my body as a third impulse again pointed me in the direction of where the dolphins might be. Once more, my hunch was correct, and the dolphins rewarded me with another jump.

With that, my reinforcement program was established, but the activity continued for what seemed like fifteen to twenty more minutes as I successfully tracked the dolphins with only two inaccurate responses. During this period, I slowly accepted the notion that the dolphins were the ones sending me these impulses and were rewarding me for my correct responses with their jumps. Once this was understood between us, they dove and didn't resurface, a behavior typical of wild dolphins anytime they have completed an interaction with someone.

As I put my binoculars away, it occurred to me that the dolphins had sent their thoughts to me much in the way a martial arts master sends the energy of his Ki in the direction of his opponent to knock him off balance. It was similar to the way it felt when the dolphins sent the energy of their sonar out ahead of them to click on things, including me and my friends, or to stun fish. In fact, experiencing the dolphins' sonar as a light-pulsing ping or tapping sensation on my skin had made me aware that they had the ability to project their energy through the water to wherever I was located—even when there was ample distance between us.

But in this case, it felt as though their ideas rather than their sonar had been sent forth and impressed upon my mind, allowing their thinking to penetrate my awareness. I also noticed that their ideas felt quite different from my own thoughts, just as the ideas sent through a radio seem distinct from my own. As I slowly absorbed the possibility that the dolphins were transmitting their ideas to me, something even more startling happened.

the dolphin garden

My first husband had just emerged from the water and suggested that we take out the kayak. As soon as we were comfortably launched and finding our paddling stride, my favorite dolphin friend began to send loud, high-pitched sounds in our direction that traveled up through the hull of our kayak and into the air. Although I couldn't see him, I turned my face toward the origin of his sound in order to chirp back, and he responded in kind. We continued to exchange chirps back and forth in this manner as we followed his sound out toward the horizon to a deeper part of the bay. He then surfaced and stopped so close to our kayak that we had to stop paddling in order to avoid hitting him.

He now remained very still beside me and looked into my eyes until I received the message to join him in the water. It felt as though I had been asked by the prince for a dance at the ball, and I began to fumble for my fins and mask as he waited patiently. Once I was in the water, he mentally invited me to perform shallow dives with him, which I did for several minutes before he slowly swam away from me and out of my sight while maintaining voice contact with me.

Next, I received a mental message to look down, and when I did I saw a dolphin garden filled with about twenty robust dolphins directly below me, all larger than the ones I had seen in the shallower part of the bay. I felt like Alice in a Wonderland of oversized dolphins that swam actively all around and under me for the next ten minutes or so. In an instant, I had entered a fantasyland and was trying to process exactly what was happening.

Meanwhile, the various dolphins began to swim by me in twos and threes and fours. It was like a promenade, and I cooed with delight as each one paraded by me. A group of about six of these large dolphins then gathered directly below me and started a spinning helix dance. I felt quite fearful as their massive, spiraling energy moved upward toward me, but to my relief, they broke out of their spin with an explosive burst of power just before hitting me. Several of them circled back to offer me eye contact and assurances that it had been a gift. A few more joined the circle, which now included "the prince," and I felt my heart expand to contain this new level of bliss. Then the dolphins left.

As I scrambled back onto the kayak, I asked my husband if he had seen what happened, and he said that he had and was simply amazed. I felt grateful for a witness to this surreal experience, and I slipped into a dreamy state as he paddled us back to shore. When we arrived, I felt compelled to write and sat on the beach scribbling an account of this mind-altering experience on a few scraps of paper. In that moment, *In the Presence of High Beings* was born.

By the end of the day, my perception of dolphins had completely shifted from seeing them as friendly and fascinating animals to viewing them as fully sentient beings. When I returned home from the bay I felt an urge to sleep that wouldn't be denied, and I surrendered to a "narcoleptic" nap. As soon as I lay down my body began to vibrate gently from within. It felt as if I was purring, and the sensation seemed strange yet pleasant, and so I fell asleep. When I awakened, the bliss lingered on within me for the next several weeks.

As I drove to my various activities over the next few days, it occurred to me that I could open my heart and send love to all of the people I passed in the same way I had learned to do with the dolphins. And so, during the following weeks, I looked at each person as a valued being crossing my path on the promenade of life and felt an urge to send love to each one. I saw that my special encounter with the dolphins in "Wonderland" had opened up this new place in my heart, and I was grateful for these feelings of love for everyone as though they were as important as my own family and self.

Yet, in spite of the power of these events, they persisted in feeling surreal. Thus, I strived over the next few years to seek both understanding and proof of what had happened. I began by reading all that I could about the nature of telepathy as well as all that humans had uncovered about how cetaceans communicate.

I discovered that the language of dolphins is not only clearly present but complex and, when investigated, seems to go well beyond ours in both sophistication and effectiveness. Moreover, it appears to operate at three levels—the physical, the telepathic, and one I would describe as symbolic or metaphoric. I also learned that these levels of communication enable dolphins to both send and receive all messages comprehensively, and that this skill prevents deceit and hidden agendas, as well as the kinds of betrayal and hurt dishonesty creates in our society. Because this level of open transmission in dolphin communication results in such seamlessly honest interactions, it serves as the foundation on which their clarity rests.

the physical level of dolphin communication

Dolphins send forth a variety of sounds, including clicks, pulses, squeaks, and whistles, which constitute what I refer to as chirping and chatter. Multiple sounds can be made, some of them simultaneously and in stereo. These sounds can travel as far as six miles and vary widely in range, often falling outside our range of hearing on both the high and low ends of the spectrum. *Ultrasound* is the term used for the high sound frequencies we can't hear, while *intrasound* is the one used for the low frequencies beyond our hearing. Each dolphin has a signature whistle that is distinct from all others and serves as his or her identification. Yet, dolphins can also imitate each others' whistles, much as humans can do impressions of other people. They are also able to imitate our laughs and words or even our accents and put this skill to good use in the interest of humor.

Although our understanding of dolphin communication is still limited, we know they bounce their sonar off various objects and receive an echo back that forms an acoustic "image" which they are then able to interpret. This ability allows them to identify small objects one hundred yards or more in the distance that we are unable to see, as well as objects behind physical barriers, including flesh and walls.

Dolphins often use this skill to identify such things as surgically placed metal pins, which seem to particularly interest them, as well as tumors that are invisible to us. For example, one woman was rammed in the chest by a captive dolphin hard enough to require a visit to her doctor, where it was discovered that she had a lung tumor she had not yet known about.

This ability to scan things out of our range of sight explains why dolphins are so interested in the abdomens of pregnant women, sometimes even before the women realize they have conceived. Once the dolphins know a woman is pregnant, they typically draw closer, send sonar to her abdomen, and seem to communicate extensively with the fetus. We were blessed to have one of these encounters last for several hours when my daughter-in-law was pregnant with my first grandchild. During that same visit, the hotel dolphins also spent generous amounts of time sending my daughter-in-law and son sonar, flirting with all of us, and repeatedly showing us how exceptionally pink their chins and bellies were, seemingly owing to the love they were sending the baby.

Research shows that dolphins not only send their sonar out to ping on things so as to read their shape, but are also able to work in tandem with each other to identify objects and respond to complex requests, even when they are separated by sound-proofed barriers. In view of these results, it is logical to assume that at the very least they are able to send information to each other.

It also appears that dolphins are able to send click-coded pictures when communicating with each other. As a result, they may not need a word or sound for objects they have identified, such as "mackerel," since they can simply transmit the sonic picture or "pictogram" of a mackerel, which can then be read by another dolphin, in a way similar to how a fax machine works. From my experience and that of others with long-term dolphin interactions, it appears that dolphins also send and read complex thoughts in a similar manner or perhaps even more directly as a transmission of thought without a need for the picture.

the telepathic layer of dolphin communication

After my special day with the binoculars and swimming in the "dolphin garden," I paid more attention to what the dolphins seemed to be saying and the way they responded to the messages I sent in return. By intensifying my observations, I hoped to confirm or deny my assumption that they had made a telepathic connection with me.

The dolphins seemed to participate in confirming the reality of telepathy between us by using a variety of ways to demonstrate that they could understand me and that I was correctly understanding them. Yet, even as they cooperated with my desire for proof, they did so in the context of their own personalities rather than mine. Consequently, their confirmations always contained an element of humor, surprise, and joy as they rewarded my correct responses or acted out their understanding of something between us. These assurances made it seem as though we were engaged in an ongoing game of charades.

For example, one day while swimming in the bay at a time when the dolphins weren't there, I felt moved by the ocean's beauty and began to hum softly into my snorkel, "He's got the whole world in His hands." Within a few minutes, about thirty dolphins unexpectedly drew near and swam beneath me in slow motion. As I continued to sing, a pair swimming directly under me caught my attention, since they were positioned precisely side-by-side rather than in the usual formation of one slightly ahead to provide a slipstream for a friend following behind. I studied them more closely to see what they were doing and noticed that their flippers were hooked together. As I puzzled over this behavior, they unhooked their flippers in slow motion and then moved them meticulously together again in order to reconnect them. With recognition, I exclaimed in my mind, "Oh, my God, are they holding hands?" With this, the pair slowly repeated their gesture and then looked at me deliberately as I laughed in acknowledgment of their communication about my song.

my search for proof

Because the concept of telepathy is not readily accepted in our culture, little has been done to investigate it, and those who explore it are often ridiculed by their peers. As a result of this cultural conditioning, no matter how clearly or often the dolphins reinforced me for my success in understanding their telepathic transmissions, I continued to struggle over whether or not I was actually talking to another species or simply sharing the zany imaginings of the famous Dr. Doolittle. To put my question to rest, I turned to research and the anecdotal experiences of others.

I discovered that even though a belief in dolphin telepathy is discouraged by most dolphinarium owners, long-standing trainers usually grow to believe in the telepathic abilities of dolphins. Ric O'Barry, trainer for the six dolphin actors who played the role of Flipper, is probably the best known of these. His view began with the fact that the dolphins he trained would often perform a trick correctly before he had given them their command, as if they were reading his mind.

Trainer Christine Bowker, who worked in Britain's first Sea World, also became a believer in telepathy when she wanted to train two dolphins to jump on either side of her and began to wonder how she could explain something so complicated to them. As soon as she completed her thought, both dolphins did exactly what she wanted and then went dashing around the pool making the funny chuckling noises dolphins often make when they are pleased with themselves.

Dean Bernal, longtime friend of the most famous sociable dolphin, Jojo, is clear that Jojo as well as the other sociable dolphins he has met in the wild communicate with him telepathically. Dean has a tape of a dolphin off the coast of Egypt kissing him after he tuned in to help her with her grief over her calf that had died.

Frank Robson, one of the early dolphin trainers at Marineland and author of *Pictures in the Dolphin Mind* (1988), believed so deeply in dolphin telepathy that he used only mental images with no whistles or food rewards in his training program. He says the dolphins responded to the requests he formed in his mind simply because they liked to please him. Robson later befriended a group of wild dolphins who also responded to the mental pictures he sent to them. And he later noticed that Horace, one of the ambassador dolphins, could sense where his group planned to take their boat and would dash to get there ahead of it and wait for it to arrive. Robson views all dolphins, both captive and free, as highly skilled in telepathy and assigns any failure to communicate with them as a lack of skill on the part of the human. I am fully aligned with Robson's observation on telepathy, and by incorporating his ideas with mine I have come up with the following guidelines for optimizing a successful exchange.

guidelines for successful telepathic transmissions

- All ideas and images sent to a dolphin must be transmitted with respect and as a request rather than a command.
- Transmissions will be successful only if the dolphin is relaxed and happy, not distracted by other things, and feels connected to the person sending the communication.
- People must clear their minds of all negative thoughts and judgments before attempting a transmission, since these are quickly received by dolphins and consistently cause them to leave an area.
- Deception is impossible with dolphins, since they receive the full truth of your thoughts and feelings rather than any false messages meant to deceive.
- To successfully communicate with dolphins, people must have good hearts, peaceful energy, and a sense of joy and play.

Yet, even when following these guidelines, Robson and other trainers who have enjoyed successful transmissions caution people not to expect dolphins to always do as you ask. Not only are they highly independent in their thinking, they regularly demonstrate their dislike of being told what to do. Moreover, they like to tease and play and will often give you what you want only after you have given up on the notion that you are in control and can get them to respond on command. In addition, they dislike repetition and often get bored with the simplistic communication most people use with them. And there are times when they are simply preoccupied by other things.

additional support for telepathy

Early in the course of my encounters with dolphins, a number of experiences suggested that they could understand me. For example, long before I considered telepathy, I was once treading water in the bay while talking to a friend about her dream of creating a dolphin-assisted healing and birthing center. I suggested she make it an open-ocean, free-access center where dolphins could do birthing and healing work voluntarily but would not be controlled in any way or fed by humans. Suddenly, five dolphins appeared out of nowhere and leaped in unison a few feet from us in a formation that resembled a chorus line. We were so startled by their nearness and size that we jumped nearly as high out of the water as they had and then laughed as they continued several more of these simultaneous broad leaps, each about five feet in length. That was the first and last we saw of the dolphins that day, but we both assumed they liked the idea of a completely free-access dolphin-assisted birthing and healing center.

I have seen dolphins do this broad leaping together on only three other occasions, and it constitutes the most powerful and dramatic behavior I have seen to date. I once saw about fifty dolphins do at least fifteen of these broad jumps consecutively, giving the impression of a show of strength in the face of something very important going on beneath the sea. Even before the concept of telepathy or symbolic language had occurred to me, it seemed that this dramatic show had been deeply meaningful in some way—although I never figured out exactly what it meant.

Further supporting my notion of dolphin telepathy, I noticed dolphins uncannily showing up for cameras, especially video cameras, and spending a good deal of time showing off in front of them. In view of the fact that research shows they intuitively understand how mirrors work and that television is a representation of reality, I wondered if they understood the purpose of cameras as well. I also noted that they seem to show up more consistently for people with good hearts, those who need healing help, those who might tell their story such as people in the entertainment business, and those who seem to be unusually wise. I further noticed that dolphins are more likely to appear whenever there are pregnant women, babies, or children in the group or when deeply injured and emotionally impaired people show up. It seemed as if they were somehow "tuned in" and ready for these connections, but I was never sure how they did it. Now telepathy offered a viable explanation for my observations.

the origins of telepathy

I learned in my search that telepathy is a natural state enjoyed between two beings in which both are able to send and receive each other's thoughts without the encumbrance of words. It is used regularly in our relationships with pre-verbal children, animals, and nature, as well as by people such as identical twins who have close bonds and open channels of communication between them. A basic understanding of telepathy explains why people may realize a family member is calling them even before the phone rings, think of an old friend a few hours before running into him, or know when someone they love is in trouble or dying.

Yet, in spite of the superiority of telepathy, we view verbal interactions as the zenith of communication and consider early verbal language in our children to be a sign of intelligence. However, if we pause to reflect, not only does verbal communication allow room for deceit and misunderstandings, it is more cumbersome and less complete than telepathy.

The truth of this was brought to my awareness when my son and his wife and I were observing a distressed dolphin obsessively twirl in circles upside down over the floor drain of his small tank. After watching spellbound for a while, we commented on how helpless we felt as our hearts went out to this troubled dolphin. The moment we expressed our concern the dolphin pulled out of his twirling and swam rapidly toward us, looking very much like a torpedo, as they do when they swim at you in this straightforward manner. Confused by this behavior, we fell silent as he approached. He then stopped within an inch of the glass separation between us, looked deeply and directly into our eyes for a moment, and then lowered his head and paused in this position before us. Within moments all three of us began at once to cry, and my sensitive daughter-in-law ran in confusion from the area. When my son and I caught up with her, we each shared that we had literally felt the intensity of the dolphin's pain within ourselves rather than as objective, albeit compassionate, observers.

It seems this dolphin had sent his insatiable feelings of loneliness, boredom, sadness, and hurt to us—much like he might send his sonar into the world. As a result, information about the dolphin's imprisonment in his painfully small pool penetrated us at a depth within ourselves impossible to glean in the course of human conversation. That moment not only provided further confirmation of how dolphins communicate but also gave us a complete and personal account of what it would be like to experience endless moments of captivity. Even though I had read well-written accounts of the agony of imprisonment, it wasn't until I actually felt this dolphin's torment within my own being, if only for a moment, that I gained a more personal understanding of just how challenging it is to lose one's freedom for hours on end, day by day, month by month, year after year. Put simply, it felt unendurable. Not only was it impossible to misinterpret this multilayered message, but our compassion and caring also went considerably deeper. I could see how this form of communication would challenge a society to be more honest, open, caring, and real. And I could see how much it would sensitize us to our oneness and the need to treat everyone fairly.

telepathy at work

Because telepathy seems to work similarly to a two-way radio or fax machine, anytime two or more parties who believe transmission is possible tune in at the same time, communication can take place.

Sometimes dolphins are tuned in when we are least expecting it. For example, when I was visiting our local marine park, a trainer was telling me about Laukani's mysterious health problems. As we were discussing her symptoms, Laukani positioned herself directly in front of us and remained there throughout our conversation while holding eye contact with me. I suggested to the trainer that she might have candidiasis, since she had low energy, an intractable skin fungus, a raw genital area with discharge, and had been on antibiotics for years. In an effort to confirm my suspicions, I asked the trainer if Laukani had symptoms of thrush in her mouth. With that, Laukani opened her mouth wide and held it open for several minutes for me to inspect. Indeed she had red, swollen gums and a bright red ring around the edges of her tongue. It was clear this dolphin knew that I had asked about her mouth and wanted me to see it. There was no trickster here, and the usually playful Laukani was serious. I wondered if she was cooperating in hopes of getting her medications corrected. The trainer later shared this information with other staff members, and I have noticed that Laukani's long-standing problem has since improved. Now, whenever I visit, she is the first to greet me, often stands upright before me in an honoring way, and gazes at me throughout my visit.

Once I learned to respect and tune in to these telepathic conversations, I began to notice upon awakening in the morning that I might sense a call to visit the dolphins that day. Each time I responded to one of these calls, no matter what time I arrived at the bay, the dolphins were in the center of it jumping to greet me. I also noticed that ideas or pictures that passed through my mind of what would take place that day often materialized.

For example, the first day I thought of taking my camera to get some photographs for the book, I received the message that the dolphins would show me their jumps only *after* I put the camera down. I thought this was an odd communication and, assuming I had mixed up the message or imagined it, I simply dismissed it and took off for the bay with my camera in tow. Yet when I arrived I found a most unusual day awaiting me. The dolphins sent me a suggestion for meeting them at the cliff where I had enjoyed some of my most interesting times with them. Prior to my awareness of the possibility of telepathy, I would have ignored this thought flowing through my head and remained at the bay. But now that I was paying attention and responding to these ideas, I headed for the cliff.

When I got there, the dolphins were waiting and seemed particularly frisky. Several executed high leaps, broad jumps, and back-flips before I could even get out of my car. I quickly gathered my gear together and set up my chair and camera in hopes of capturing these unusual shots. But once I was prepared, the jumps ceased abruptly, and the dolphins remained silently beneath the water. I sat for a long time with my camera poised, waiting for a surprise jump. But none came, and the water remained unusually still. Eventually, I assumed the dolphins had left since they weren't even coming up for air, and I rested my camera in my lap. The moment I did this, the leaps began again. When I picked up my camera, the activity ceased. I soon realized I was being teased and began to chuckle. This went on for another twenty minutes before I remembered that this game had been foretold earlier that morning.

The consistency of this playful game and the dolphins' merciless teasing got me laughing aloud as I pleaded for at least one shot. Although I didn't get a single picture, I drove home with a big smile on my face. I had gone to visit the dolphins in spite of a busy schedule that day because I felt a little low, and I left filled with endorphins and a parting message from the dolphins that the elevated feelings had been more important than the pictures. Besides, they were teaching me to be more dolphin-like and playful rather than so serious and goal-oriented as humans are prone to be. This is a consistent message delivered from the dolphins in a variety of ways, and they often send me home laughing and joyful in lieu of helping me meet my goals—even when my projects include helping them in some way.

On another day, I felt pulled to the cliff again and when I arrived, twenty dolphins were gathered at its base quietly bobbing up and down. Once I was settled into my beach chair with my camera poised, the dolphins began to jump and play, so I tried to capture a shot of them. Just as I noticed how hard it was to see a jump, aim the camera, and get a picture, a message was transmitted for me to simply point the camera at a place on the water and the dolphins would jump into my sight, just as they had with my binoculars. I was skeptical and assumed I had made up this idea but tried it anyway. When I then pointed my camera randomly, the dolphins leaped repeatedly into my sight, and I was able to capture about fifteen jumps, though I lacked the proper equipment or skill and all of them were quite small.

Next, I began to wonder how I would get a shot of the high leap I envisioned for my cover. Almost immediately, a dolphin leaped twenty feet into the air right in front of me, portraying the image of the cover I had in my mind. Prior to this I had seen dolphins jump this high on only a few rare occasions in the open ocean, so I sat stunned for a while absorbing this profound communication between us. Unfortunately, it happened so quickly I failed to respond in time to capture it on film.

When I was on a boat trip several months later, I was telepathically reminded of this technique for photographing dolphin jumps and captured several good shots. That same day, a young dolphin kept waving his tail at one of our guests who seemed somewhat perplexed by our belief in their telepathy. Every time one of us mentioned this connection between our friend and the dolphin, the dolphin would wave his tail again until he got us all laughing, including our guest.

Taking any one of these events in isolation would not cause anyone to conclude that dolphins are telepathic, but when this small sampling of my larger collection of stories is lumped together, it becomes a challenge to hold on to the idea that dolphins do not possess this ability. The reason that trusting in it is so important to an understanding of dolphins is that the thorough communication telepathy affords lays the foundation on which their honesty and clarity are built.

Yet, even with so much proof of the validity of telepathy, I continued to want more, especially because telepathy has been pushed so far outside the realm of reality for our society that even when I repeatedly experienced it, I had trouble believing in its truth. And like Alice in Wonderland, I felt a need for additional reassurances that the world before me was real.

bubbles

Thus, to my own puzzlement, even though telepathic experiences occurred on a regular basis, I continued to question them. Then one day, a dolphin reinforced me with the gift of a bubble for understanding a message he had delivered. Not only was I delighted by the bubble, it seemed like the perfect way to communicate to me in a concrete way that I had succeeded in understanding his telepathic message. Following this event, I became enchanted by bubbles and always pleaded for more as a way to confirm a telepathic transmission between us. Yet, even when I succeeded in eliciting one, I would ask for another. Over time, this became my favorite symbol of understanding between us, and each time I received the gift of a bubble, I felt as though the dolphins had recognized and connected with me.

Consequently, when a friend invited me to join her for a week of swimming with the dolphins on the Big Island, I sent out a request for bubbles. I also asked to play the leaf game since this was the island where the game had originated. This was my first time swimming with these dolphins, and I was delighted to see them playing in the bow wave of our boat as we headed out to sea our first morning. After a while the dolphins slowed down and began to circle our boat, prompting the captain to cut his speed. Next, they drew closer, requiring him to go even slower, and then they completely stopped, indicating a desire to swim with us. One of them positioned himself alongside the boat next to me with a garbage bag on his tail, which I assumed was in response to my request to play the passing game. He watched me gather my gear together as he deftly moved his bag from his tail to his dorsal fin, then to his flipper, and finally back to his tail.

Unfortunately, I was distracted from our game when, upon entering the water, I felt unexpected fear as I realized I couldn't see the bottom, which fell hundreds of feet away from me in the seamless, open ocean. Instantly, five dolphins gathered about ten feet under me, forming a temporary floor for me to look at, and hung there until I settled down. This gesture quickly calmed my anxiety, and I have not felt uncomfortable in such depth of ocean since.

As these dolphins moved away from my floor arrangement, one released a large bubble that floated directly up to me. When I squealed with delight, he released another, and when I squealed again, he sent one more. It seemed these dolphins had in fact heard my requests and were responding without the same reserve or teasing I endured from the Oahu dolphins. Interestingly, once we were back on board, the guides exclaimed that they had not previously seen so many bubbles nor such large ones in any one encounter.

the symbolic level of dolphin communication

Since bringing things from the ocean that we have requested is a good way for free dolphins to prove their telepathic skills, they often respond to a call for debris, which they swish back and forth on their tails or hang on their fins as they prance by or beneath us while holding playful eye contact. One dolphin is even reported to have acted out a socially conscious message by returning with a garbage bag after being asked what she wanted to do for Earth Day.

I had seen a video of my friend Joan Ocean (*Dolphins into the Future*, 1997) playing the leaf game with the dolphins on the Big Island and had thought of introducing this game to the Oahu dolphins. Then one day, while at the bay, I remembered this idea and began to search in the water for a suitable leaf or object to pass back and forth. Since there is very little foliage at the bay, I was able to find only a small leaf floating along the surface, which I picked up to examine but rejected as too small and returned to the water.

A little later a dolphin swam directly under me with a couple of his friends. He was bobbing his head up and down in an exaggerated manner that caused me to wonder what might be wrong with him. Upon closer examination, it looked as though he had a small hook caught in his mouth, and I was trying to figure out how I might help him release it. He then slowly rose from the depths to a position directly beneath me and, as he passed by, turned his head to show me that he was holding something between his lips. A shiver ran through my body when I realized that it was a leaf, a very small leaf, perhaps the one I had just returned to the water. This dolphin had clearly overheard my thoughts about the passing game and was demonstrating his ability to hold the small leaf in his mouth. Unfortunately I was so distracted by this display that I didn't think to suggest that he pass it to me in order to continue the game.

Another time, after the spinner dolphins had spent hours scanning my daughter-in-law's pregnant belly, she said aloud to the group in general, "I've been showing you my belly all morning. How about you showing me yours?" With that, one of the dolphins positioned himself upright directly before her and my son, and then from that position beneath the surface he began to spiral himself all the way out of the water into a spinning jump. Not only had he shown her his stomach, he had joyfully raised the level of the game—a very dolphin-like quality.

a world alive with communion

Although it took me a while to trust in the telepathy of dolphins, once I accepted the possibility of such a phenomenon, it opened up a whole new world alive with conversation. After I tuned in, it wasn't long before I noticed that the fish in the ocean were also responsive to the energies I sent to them, as were the turtles and the rays. In fact, whenever I would consciously send waves of love from my heart out into the ocean in an effort to attract dolphins, these other friends would often turn off their course and swim over to me.

I have similarly observed butterflies and birds and others on land responding to the energies of love when actively sent to them and have noticed that telepathic transmissions work with domesticated animals as well. In fact, one amusing story surfaced during a dinner party with friends. I had fallen instantly in love with their darling German Shepherd, who was sitting between me and his adored mistress under the dinner table as we talked into the night. Eventually, the dog began to look at me as if to ask if we would ever stop talking, so I threw some thoughts his way to keep him better entertained and more included in our conversation. Knowing he wanted to get to bed, one of my thoughts was, "Do you ever sleep in the bed with your mistress and master?" Since I was a houseguest, the following morning when I joined the family for breakfast, his mistress greeted me with consternation over the fact that he had jumped onto their bed that night, something he had never done before. I told her about the thought I had transmitted, and because she already believed her dog to be telepathic, my confession solved this mystery for her.

Once we become aware of telepathy, it offers an explanation as to how dogs and cats and even pigs and other pets in the news have been able to tune in to their owner's need for help or a telepathic request to bring them a telephone. It also explains how the famous parrot Alex, given enough vocabulary to express himself, has been able to share more than we dreamed possible for a bird, even indicating when he has had enough of a training session and wants a shower and his supper. And it explains how Koko, the famed signing gorilla, is able to include herself in a conversation between others that is devoid of any signing. It also explains how she once expressed compassion for a horse carrying a rider along the roadside whose "mouth hurt" because of "something" in it. It also explains a number of telepathic communications taking place in the plant world, which numerous studies have validated, including extensive ones done by Cleve Baxter, as described in *Primary Perception*, which is finally gaining acceptance by scientists from major universities. In fact, Baxter's studies go so far as to establish the conscious response of things like eggs in a room getting excited when other eggs are being broken and cooked.

If birds and dogs and pigs and plants can tune in to the collective discussion, surely the large-brained dolphins and whales are able to communicate intuitively. There is clearly a conversation in our midst that we have not been privy to as a result of our belief that we are the only ones able to converse. What a surprise to discover that the other species are not only communicating within their own groups but with each other as well and have probably been eavesdropping on us to boot.

How embarrassing to learn after all this time that we are possibly the only ones who have been excluded from this collective conversation while everyone else is in on the secret. Ironically, our pomposity has walled us off from this rich and delightful connection between others living in our world, and the joke is on us. Will we be able to set aside our pride in order to tune in late, or will we fight tooth and nail to continue to ridicule and discount this delightful conversation going on around us? If we open to it, we will discover a loving and joyful world right under our noses. For once we are tuned in, we become aware of our connection to others, our compassion is deepened, and our caring and love are activated and expanded.

the cost of denying our telepathy

It is interesting that our babies and young children are initially adept at telepathy but lose this ability because of our cultural disbelief in this high-level skill and failure to use it. In fact, when I first became aware that animals could receive my messages, I began to notice a similar response in babies and young children who would turn to look my way and smile whenever I sent them a message or an extra surge of love.

Many mothers are aware of this telepathic connection with their infants and respond to their silent calls as part of their early communication process. And most of us are aware that telepathy between mother and child is especially clear during times of emergency when the messages sent by children in need are strong and clear and are less likely to be doubted or ignored.

Yet, these early transmissions are later discounted, and parents stop listening or responding to them. As a result, we stop communicating directly with our children in this way, often look to others for answers to their needs, and allow this rich opportunity to understand and know each other at the heart of our truths to go virtually untapped and unused.

Telepathy is not only ignored in our culture but scorned if not feared as occult in nature. As a result, we have lost our awareness of this aspect of communication, and our failure to use it has caused this skill to atrophy in most of us. Some speculate that this once-natural method of communication has been lost owing to our growing desire to hide our less honorable motives, as commerce and the desire to get ahead of others have developed. Yet, exclusively verbal communication has not only cut us off from deeper conversations with each other, it has created a serious separation of our hearts from nature and others with whom we share this planet.

telepathy serving truth and clarity

Once I opened to telepathic communication, I realized how easily it exposes hidden thoughts and agendas, as well as deceit and betrayal so common in our language-dependent species. I could also see that reclaiming this skill would force humans to be more honest and offer a fuller understanding of each other. This would in turn allow us to feel safer and, thus, closer to one another and to move beyond our unkind and self-serving ways to create a kinder, more loving, and harmonious society.

I first noticed how this might work after swimming with the dolphins for several hours one day. I was getting cold and a little bored but didn't feel free to get out of the water until the dolphins left. The moment I had this thought, the happy chirping and chatter of the dolphins stopped abruptly as though a symphony conductor had closed his fingers on the end of a score. The dolphins then left the area and didn't return for the remainder of the day. I realized instantly that they had received my thought, and I felt badly that they had eavesdropped on my boredom. Accompanying their departure was the message impressed in my mind that humans have trouble focusing for very long on pleasure and prefer to focus on their chores and problems. Because of this tendency, it was gently suggested that people would be wise to develop a greater tolerance for joy.

Following this experience, I noticed that the dolphins would also leave the area anytime my thoughts became the least bit judgmental. For example, I had traveled long and far to see the small group of dolphins at Tin Can Bay in Australia, and I felt blessed when the primary mother and her calf showed up just as we arrived. However, as the calf surfaced to take a frontal peek and then swam directly toward me, I thought to myself how odd he looked. He was a different variety from that of the dolphins I was used to seeing, and his direct approach made him look quite peculiar. The moment this unseemly thought escaped my mind, the young calf dove his head underwater as if ashamed to be viewed any further and quickly turned to swim away. I felt terrible and would have given anything to take back that careless moment of judgment.

I had a similar experience with a lone dolphin riding our boat's bow wave in Australia's Harvey Bay. He appeared after a pair of whales had startled us into hollers of joy with a surprise tandem breach within a few feet of our boat, followed by two hours of more breaches, spy-hops (eye-at-the-surface peeks at the world), and pectoral and tail slaps and waves. After this magnificent show, the lone dolphin appeared in our bow wave as our boat turned to head for the harbor. The contrast of his smallness to the whales' larger-than-life performance triggered a thought of how insignificant he seemed when compared to the immense and wonderful whales. He immediately impressed on me the sadness he felt as he dove out of our bow wave, never to return. I carried the hurt of these two dolphins in my heart for a long time, allowing it to serve as a worthy reminder of the pain my judgments create for others.

It also became clear to me following these events that our judgments go out into the atmosphere and affect others, even when we think they are private. Psychics have seen and described this energy for years, and, more recently, bioenergy photos of energy fields around both animate and inanimate objects are making this previously unseen reality visible for all to see. Dr. Masaru Emoto also shows us the visible impact our thoughts have on our environment with his photographs of beautiful crystals frozen from water that has been sent kind and loving messages in contrast to ugly photographs of water unable to even crystallize after being scorned and scolded.

The departure on the part of the hurt dolphins served as a reminder that my thoughts are not only known to the dolphins but are naked in the telepathic universe. Following this lesson, I realized one day not only that I was accountable for all of my thoughts but that they were capable of starting a pattern of negative energy in myself as well as in others around me. I realized it would be a wise idea to clean them up and live as if everyone was as telepathic as the dolphins. This guideline has served me well in my subsequent interactions with others, and because it has inspired me to live only by my truth, it has also served as a key to my personal growth and freedom.

truth as the only path to clarity

As I personally experienced the growth and freedom that go with the level of honesty required for a telepathic society, I became aware of how deeply a lack of truth has penetrated our culture and seems to lie at the core of our problems. It has become equally clear that bringing the truth back at the level telepathy requires would be the best prescriptive for our society and world.

In contrast to our pervasively deceptive human culture, dolphins live in an open society where there are no secrets and all motives are exposed to the group. Thus, if one member does something disruptive or unsupportive of the group, the others know about it and band together to discipline him. This prevents dolphins from manipulating others, developing ongoing patterns of disruptive behaviors, or secretly working against the needs of the larger group. In this way, telepathy enables dolphins to interrupt all negative patterns and prevent entrainment to behaviors counter to the needs of the pod.

a conversation beneath the sea

Once we develop awareness of conversations among species as well as between them, our universe becomes more animated and alive. When we also learn from new breakthroughs in quantum physics that we all share a unified mind, or common space called "the field," where all of our thoughts and our consciousness live, we can see how easily these conversations can reach out and be overheard by others both nearby and far away.

This understanding explains the claim people make that once you have swum with dolphins, other dolphins from different parts of the world will recognize you. It's as if the dolphins use a telepathic link along the network of shared space for broader communication, and this same link may be what the whales use to communicate the song they will sing each year. It may also be the link psychic people are able to tune into to know things outside the awareness of others not tuned in to it.

Even before hearing this, I had noticed that wherever I traveled, the dolphins and whales in each area seemed to greet me with recognition. They also consistently presented me with bubbles as if they were calling cards they knew I would recognize and enjoy. In fact, over time it seemed as though the primary way dolphins from all over the world used to convince me that I understood their thoughts was to send me bubbles—big bubbles, small bubbles, ringed bubbles, and cloud bubbles. But I was insatiable and would always ask for even more bubbles to be sent, since I longed for additional proof, and the bubbles anchored me in something tangible and real in the midst of this otherwise surreal experience of communicating with another species.

Yet, even though the dolphins responded, they did so in their own playful and unpredictable manner, preferring to tease and surprise me with unexpected behaviors in order to evoke joy rather than comply with my desire for predictability and control. Thus, although the cherished bubbles came in many sizes and shapes and from dolphins all over the world, they always came on the dolphins' terms rather than mine. This unpredictable delivery of the bubbles added to their magic and my delight, and I came to view them as wonderfully precious gifts. Yet no matter how many bubbles the dolphins sent, my doubts about their role in confirming a communication between us persisted.

Then one day, I felt compelled to visit our local dolphinarium in order to connect with the dolphins that had been moved from the hotel. When I arrived at the park's central dolphin tank, a female named Laka swam over to greet me. As I asked a trainer about where I might find the hotel dolphins, Laka engaged me in a prolonged gaze. I was enjoying this encounter and felt rather special and chosen when the trainer informed me that Laka was the dominant dolphin in this tank. In fact, as Laka continued our unbroken gaze, the trainer explained how the staff had recently discovered that when the other dolphins weren't cooperating, it was often because Laka had ordered them not to comply. Sadly, they used this information to often separate Laka from the others.

As I gazed back at Laka, I discerned a slight shift move through her body and a naughty twinkle light up her eye. Just as I was trying to understand what was going on, she splashed me with a sizable wall of water. I was shocked and looked down at my clothes to find that she had completely drenched me. I quickly looked back at Laka in time to see her entire face light up as her eyes flashed gleefully back into mine. I couldn't help but burst out laughing. Laka then surprised me again by mimicking my laugh, which made me laugh even harder. Next, Laukani joined in the fun from a nearby tank with her own imitation of my laugh, and I laughed even harder still, as did both dolphins until the three of us got downright hysterical.

After I recovered from this very dolphin-like encounter, the trainer took me downstairs to watch the dolphins from the underwater observation station. The moment we got to the curved surveillance window, Laka was there waiting for us. I put my hand on the window, and Laka nuzzled her cheek into my hand from the other side of the bubble. She remained there, gazing at me while the trainer and I talked. I returned Laka's steady gaze as I conversed with the trainer about the program.

When there was an opportunity for questions, I asked if the captive dolphins blew bubbles in their pool like the ones in the open ocean do. The moment my question was framed, Laka released an enormous bubble. Even the trainer, who did not believe in dolphin telepathy, was briefly startled by this gesture but then recomposed herself and continued with her description of the program. I was thrilled by Laka's public demonstration of understanding between us, and I hoped to draw more of the trainer's attention to what had just happened. So I looked at Laka and said aloud, "You heard me ask about the bubbles, didn't you?" Maintaining our steady gaze, Laka now answered with a twinkle that danced in her eye. Realizing the observation area was probably being taped, I asked aloud for more bubbles. She hesitated for a few moments and then, with a mischievous glint in her eye, produced a stream of the tiniest bubbles imaginable. I laughed again at how this very funny dolphin had found a way to respond and yet achieve control under circumstances that afforded her very little opportunity to do so.

Later, as I prepared to leave this area to search for my hotel friends and was saying my good-byes to Laka, I silently asked for one more bubble, which she released along with a soulful, less mischievous gaze. Tears spilled down my cheeks as I walked away, my heart filled with emotion. Not only had I enjoyed this delicious encounter with the funny Laka, I knew once and for all that the dolphins understood and communicated with me.

Even more poignant was the fact that this proud and dominant dolphin had surrendered to my requests for bubbles in the presence of a third party. Although the trainer had been conditioned not to look for telepathic communication or to attach too much importance to it, she had noticed. Even more important, I was finally convinced that the dolphins and I were in fact holding a conversation beneath the sea. It had taken me ten years and many bubbles to surrender to this concept. And I was grateful to Laka for finally getting through. Accepting this interspecies communication through the common language of telepathy opened up my own world in a new way, and I could see that if humanity would trust in this skill and develop it ourselves, we could easily live with as much honesty, openness, and clarity on land as the dolphins enjoyed beneath the sea.

The late Dr. David Viscott taught that our mental illness and mental health lie along the same continuum as our honesty and secrets. Thus, the greater our truth, the greater our health, and the greater our deception, the greater our illness. Truth has been slipping away in our society, and our mental health has slipped away with it. Now we have a way to bring the truth back and our mental health with it. We need only to do what the dolphins do—trust our intuition and truth, and then tune in and use it.

By not listening to our own hearts or the hearts of others, we have failed to hear either the song or the cries of the world around us and have become insensitive to its needs as well as its joys. Consequently, we no longer see value in the lives of other humans or the animals in our midst, much less in the flowers and trees. This results in our trampling over everyone outside of ourselves in pursuit of our own comfort and pleasure.

This loss of bonding and connection to one another, combined with a lack of honesty and honor, is the price we have paid for losing our telepathic skills. As these breaks in our bonds deepen, deceit creeps relentlessly into all aspects of our society, putting our mental health and clarity dangerously at risk. A return to our belief in telepathy and deep, sensitive listening can bring it back. To begin, we must put our superiority and pride aside, then get still, and listen. If we take this step, we will be surprised by the breadth of the conversation in our midst and the love for others we will feel when we tune in to it.

As I left the area, I silently promised Laka that I would put aside my embarrassment about telepathy and talking to dolphins. I would not only claim my own intuitive skills but would tell the story of the dolphins' sentient nature, their intelligence, and their special brand of joyful wisdom. And I would come out of my closet of fear about broadcasting the secrets they had shared regarding how humanity can also live with the wisdom, love, harmony, and joy found only through the kind of clarity and truth attainable in a seamlessly honest world.

clarity is achieved through complete and honest communications that bring us all the way out of the shadows and into the light.

the sixth gift:

mastery and grace woven into all aspects of life

Spin and weave the wondrous dance of mastery and grace.

Once I was able to communicate more deeply with the dolphins, I discovered that the real magic was not how they communicated but what they were saying.

As I paid more attention to the dolphins' message, I realized they were not only showing me their own embodiment of the six traits of the higher self but were also instructing me in how to act as my own higher self. They were also showing me a surprisingly clear and simple formula for manifesting a life filled with joy while creating the world of my dreams, which I describe in Part 3.

I also noticed that they seemed to be disclosing increasingly deeper concepts by using a combination of acting out more complicated metaphors and impressing complex ideas upon my awareness. These began with the complexity of their bubble sculptures and ability to construct vortexes, helices, and torus bubbles, as well as their acting out a spiraling helix spin during swims with me. In addition to these structures, they repeatedly showed me that they could send a strong force of implosive, rather than explosive, energy out ahead of them and would even give each other rides in these fields of energy. It also seemed that they were able to extend the forward movement of this energy from a non-visible place within them, rather than the external movements we are used to seeing when things are in motion.

When I inquired about the deeper meaning of these metaphoric representations, I was given an impression of complex ideas along with the suggestion that there were scientists who could more easily unravel what the dolphins were portraying if I would share these activities and my impressions. Interestingly, during the time between the first and second editions of this book, I learned more about what I was seeing, and it became apparent that most of the dolphins' structures and concepts were included in the emerging quantum unified field theories most clearly expressed in the book *The Field,* by Lynn McTaggert, and the wonderful film *What the Bleep Do We Know?* Others are still being discussed and explored by some of our brightest scientists.

In addition to the concepts revealed in this book and film, I wondered if the dolphins were also using their bubble vortexes and helix spins to act out a demonstration of how our DNA strands serve as the building blocks of creation. I wondered, for example, if whatever we energetically plant in the petrie dishes of our hearts and personal energy fields is what we will grow more of in the same way that DNA put in a petrie dish in a science lab produces more of its own likeness. I further wondered if, once a pattern is selected and grown, it also serves as a magnet—or antenna—that draws more of the selected energy back to it.

I also wondered if they were partnering with other scientific discoveries that reveal how this spiraling force of life is not only powered by the energy of love and joy but also slows down or stops when compassion and caring fail to flow through its energetic pathway. If so, could this be their reminder to humanity to work more sincerely at becoming a genuinely compassionate, loving, and joyful species?

Are the dolphins suggesting, as some of our scientists do, that we have the capacity to choose what we want to grow more of and draw back to us? Are they also showing us that by using this information it really wouldn't be all that hard to influence evolutiaonary changes in our DNA and create the lives of our dreams?

Are they showing us that the way to achieve this next level of our evolution is by embracing compassion and love as the quiet, yet enormously powerful forces that fuel the spiraling nature of all life from the tiniest photon to the greatest galaxies?

Are they reminding us with their torroidal bubbles and spinning dances that all that we are is built on the foundation of this spiraling force driven by the sweetness of love and power of joy as they flow through our hearts to empower our lives whenever we act as our higher selves?

And is it this same spiraling power of love that gracefully twirls the whales into soft pirouettes beneath the sea and then thrusts their massive tonnage spiraling into the air, perhaps attracting their females with the power of their love rather than their force, as we have assumed?

Is it this same strength of love that enables dolphins to generate spiraling bands of healing sonar and twirl multiple times through the air, visibly throwing their healing, love, and joy into the world and drawing it back to themselves?

These were the impressions I received while pondering my questions about the dolphins' spiraling structures, coupled with the idea that if I share them with others, they will serve as leads for scientists to explore. In addition to this repeating spiraling theme, the dolphins produced what appears to be sonoluminescence in the bay, or the heating of bubbles with sonar to a temperature that causes them to glow. Some scientists believe this may be connected to cold fusion and could perhaps be used as a powerful energy source.

the mastery of teaching and the teaching of mastery

I further realized that the dolphins were speaking through me as an author to a wider audience in order to show humanity how to achieve the same kind of grace on land as they had achieved beneath the sea. Once I understood that the dolphins were acting as instructors, I could see how uniquely qualified they were to teach us about the higher self and to share their insights for manifesting our dreams. Not only had they consistently acted as their higher selves during the ten years I had known them, but they also seemed to have manifested a species and world filled with wisdom, love, harmony, and joy in their watery domain.

Following this realization, it became clear that the dolphins' sixth and most important trait was the gift of mastery, a quality achieved only by those who live in a constant state of love, while taking heaven with them wherever they go.

By modeling their gifts of the higher self and teaching their insights for manifesting miracles, the dolphins are offering humanity a formula for healing our hearts and creating the world of our dreams. Thus, we need only to recognize these lessons and apply them if we wish to achieve the same state of harmony on our shores as the dolphins have achieved below them. To begin, we can weave the six gifts of character the dolphins embody into our own molecular structure and DNA. We can then add the six insights for manifestation they teach,m as presented in the following section.

By embracing these intertwining qualities deep within ourselves, we can weave loving clarity and joy into our hearts and all that we do as a gift to ourselves and our shared earth. Not only would this fulfill our collective mission of bringing heaven to earth, but our hearts would also be free to join the dolphins in their dance of mastery and grace.

dance your way to
heaven on earth.

PART 3

creating the world
of your dreams
six insights for manifesting goals

the first insight:

select and yearn for your dreams

Send thoughts filled with dreams ahead to prepare the way for your future.

Once telepathy between us was established, I became aware that the dolphins were teaching me a number of valuable lessons about how to live life with as much magic and joy as they do. Not only were they modeling the six personality traits of the higher self, they had six insights to share about how humanity could manifest their dreams.

Yet, it wasn't until I began to organize the material and write this book that the six lessons popped out as a clear and easy recipe for manifesting our personal and shared goals. Only then could I see that the dolphins were showing me not only how I could act as my higher self and make my personal dreams come true, but also how humanity as a whole could function as a more evolved species and join together to create a world of our dreams.

early clues to dolphin magic

My awareness that the dolphins would serve as my teachers began the day my dolphin guide first "danced" with me in the "dolphin garden." Like Alice in her Wonderland, I not only realized as we glided through the water together that my experience was getting "curiouser and curiouser," but that it was also getting deeper and more interesting. I had my first glimpse during this experience that I was being shown a series of lessons on how we can manifest the things we desire.

Upon arriving home, I fell into a deep sleep, and it wasn't until I awakened refreshed that I pondered what I had learned to date. In doing this, I noticed that a number of the lessons had been delivered at the beginning of our relationship, but that there were more to come. At this point, I realized that something big was happening, yet I didn't know what.

Over the next few years, six simple lessons were delightfully presented and repeatedly restated and reinforced. These lessons were very different from any I had acquired from other sources and showed me in a new way for humans to act as their higher selves while manifesting the world of their dreams. Each lesson stood alone and worked well. Yet, when used together, they proved to be life-changing.

What surprised me was how the dolphins' lessons for manifesting seemed both similar to and different from other formulas I had learned. Yet, even in the areas where they were similar, they seemed much simpler to understand and follow than the others had been. When I later tried them, it was the first time I was able to succeed in consciously manifesting something I desired.

the first lessons

Once I understood that the dolphins were acting as teachers, I realized that some of their lessons had been introduced during my initial encounters with them. In those early days, I was taught to more clearly *claim and yearn for what I wanted* and then to *show up for the experience* while *finding a way to remain attractive* in order to draw it to me.

As I began to write these insights down, it became clear that each insight for how to manifest our dreams intertwined with the others. Yet for the sake of clarity, I have separated them into six separate insights.

select and yearn for your dreams

In this first insight, the dolphins emphasized the need to *clearly select and then yearn for your dream while calling it to you with your heart.* This lesson was revealed to me in the following way.

When I first selected the dream of swimming with dolphins and began to call them to me, I was made aware that it was the strength of my yearning for the dream that had set things in motion and had served as a more critical step in making it happen than I initially realized. Yet, at its beginning stages, this dream was diffuse and not something I desired or yearned for. In fact, it began as an item on a long list of things I dreamed of doing someday. As a result, it had started to unfold in an undirected manner, in proportion to the place it had on my list. Consequently, the dream didn't begin to come into focus or find its way to me until years later, when the desire for it increased.

Yet, even when my interest intensified and the dream drew closer, my desire was still not as strong as it needed to be to bring it to fruition. The dolphins made me aware of this lack of clarity and strength of desire regarding my wish to swim with them when they showed up at a beach I was scouting with some friends in preparation for a larger group plan to swim with them the following day. Because the dolphins' early arrival was not on my schedule and our other friends were enjoying a tennis round-robin at the hotel where we were staying, I elected to return to the hotel to play tennis. Besides, I assumed the dolphins would return the following day, when everyone would be there to enjoy the experience.

However, the next morning when we arrived at the bay bright and early, we could hear the dolphins chirping, but they never showed their faces or let us see or play with them. Of course, I had missed the dolphins the previous day in order to play tennis. Yet, after I had returned to the hotel and joined my friends on the court, my desire to play had not been strong enough to engage enthusiastically or play well. The next day, as I floated in the bay in search of dolphins, it occurred to me that I had failed to succeed in either tennis or swimming with the dolphins. And I could see that I needed to increase the strength of my desire for things, since half-hearted involvement in activities was not rewarding.

After that weekend, I decided more clearly to claim my desire to swim with the dolphins, and I vowed that I would succeed. As a result, my longing to connect with them increased, and it wasn't long before this dream was fulfilled.

Biophysicist Candace Pert (*Molecules of Emotion*, 1997) explains how this works, even at the molecular level. She discovered in her work that once a desire or yearning for something is set in motion, our receptor molecules work together with rhythmic, vibrating ligands to create a tango between them, one as the yearner and the other as the responder. When we view this dance of courtship between our molecules under a microscope, we can see how at the very core of our biochemistry we attract and pull to us those things we desire. Since, in order to do this, our receptors must shape themselves to attract and hook things that are compatible to them, it's essential to let them know what you want rather than confuse them by focusing on what you don't want or with vague requests.

Thus, if you clearly fill your heart with the energy and yearning for love, love receptors will chemically respond and form a specific shape designed to attract and hook the essence of love to you. Likewise, when you are filled with the energy and intensity of anger meant for others, your receptors shape themselves to attract and hook anger to you. Consequently, if you want love in your life, it's important to fill your heart with the desire and energy of love. Similarly, if you want to swim with dolphins, it's important to fill your heart with an intense yearning for this.

Coupling this information with the results of the Princeton Engineering Anomalies Research (PEAR) experiments, designed to measure the impact of our desires and intentions on the world, shows us how the power of our desires influences others to respond. The increasingly recognized PEAR study program based at Princeton University has demonstrated that the intention or strong desire of an individual can influence the outcome. For example, an alternate intention sent to a randomly programmed machine is able to influence the machine to respond to the intention of the operator, rather than its original program. These results suggest that our desires and the receptor hooks they create are able to exert their influence beyond our own bodies and draw the things we want from the world to us. This matches the research reported in Larry Dossey's *Healing Words* (1993) and other works.

It also explains why sending a strong wave of energy carrying our desires, prayers, beliefs, and intentions out into the world has such a powerful influence on the world, as well as on what comes back to us. Accordingly, once I selected swimming with dolphins as a clear and strong desire, not only did my intention broadcast the call for this experience into the world, but my receptor hooks prepared themselves to attract and receive it. Before long, we made a connection. This is visually demonstrated in the film, "What the Bleep Do We Know?"

Interestingly, as a desired event or type of person is yearned for, the object's own yearning can also become activated, causing the two to be drawn even more magnetically toward the other. In my case, the dolphins not only came to me as a result of my yearning for them but also later called me to them as well. In fact, it was their strong call to me that compelled me to look through my binoculars as the dolphins jumped into my sights and later to follow the sounds of my dolphin guide out to the "dolphin garden." I realized from the viewpoint of being the one called and yearned for how powerful the urge to respond can be, especially when the call of the yearner is sent with the force the dolphins possess.

I periodically wondered why the dolphins had chosen me to call in this way and concluded that it was because I was an intuitive yet credible counselor and author who had access to swimming regularly with them for as long as needed to learn the lessons they would teach me. After I had been put on the receiving end of this selection and calling process, I could feel the dolphins pulling me to the bay on many occasions. Whenever I went on the days I felt this pull, they were invariably there waiting to interact. Whenever I didn't go, I felt uneasy all day and was often told by other swimmers how special that day had been.

Being on the receiving end of the dolphins' yearning made me aware that if I called people and events to me in the same strong, sustained manner, they too would be on the receiving end of my intense yearning. As the dolphins made me aware, this is an active rather than a passive process, and I must first declare exactly what I am selecting and then clearly and strongly call it to me.

This call and response process works very well and is an important component of the magic of creation. Yet, it only works if you are careful to hold only those things in your mind and heart that are in alignment with your higher self and that you genuinely wish to draw to you.

clear selections

Now that we understand how our intense focus on something will bring it to us, we must be mindful of where we are putting our attention. Since most people give more energy and attention to what they don't want than to what they would like to have, their minds often wander into the past as they fester over earlier poor decisions and events in an effort to repair them or wish them away. Or they drift into the future with worries about what might happen. Even when their thoughts are in the present, they may have doubts and fears about their ability to fulfill their dreams. Or they may be filled with feelings of irritation with themselves and others or hope that their friends won't succeed too abundantly or that their enemies will fail.

Yet, just as our longing for a dream pulls the dream to us, putting our attention on our regrets and worries or ill will toward others will pull those very energies to us as well. In fact, awareness of how this works explains how the laws of karma or cause and effect are fulfilled. It also explains how bad things can happen to good people who focus on their doubts and fears rather than on their faith in their ability and right to attract abundance and joy. And it explains how grace is set in motion: For in the moment when we deeply yearn to hold the energies of nonjudgment, forgiveness, and love for others in our hearts, we draw those energies of goodwill to ourselves as well.

This is why whatever intentions you place in your heart, whether for good or bad fortune for yourself or others, will eventually find their way to you. Because the dolphins understand this concept, they clearly select only loving energies to hold in their hearts and send forth to others at all times. The love and joy they bring to the world as a result of this choice offers testimony to the power of yearning for our own immersion in love and joy.

yearn only for good for
yourself and others.

the second insight:

show up for your dreams

Get on the path of your dreams and meet them there.

The second insight is best described *as the need to show up in order to be on the path of your dreams when they arrive.* This idea was initially presented during the period when I was first trying to connect with the dolphins and was later repeated and reinforced on many other occasions.

Although I didn't notice this lesson when it was first presented, once I realized it was one of the dolphins' insights, I could see how failing to show up for my dreams had been a factor in my life. As the dolphins made me more alert to this pattern, I noticed a cluster of reasons why people like myself resist showing up.

One day I felt called to go to the bay and, as a result of my earlier lesson, wanted to be sure to show up for whatever might happen. As soon as I arrived and entered the water, a young dolphin established voice contact with me. Yet, although he called back and forth to me the entire time I was in the water, the dolphins never came near enough for me to see or play with them. After a while, I got cold and, giving up on an encounter, swam for shore. When I got there, the dolphins broke into a chorus of chatter and gave me the message that I needed to stretch myself more. Thus, despite the cold and extra exercise, I swam back out. Yet, once I got there, I continued to be teased and was lured into swimming even further.

After staying with the program for longer than I usually would, I was rewarded with a particularly special swim with the dolphins. As I watched them circle me for the next forty-five minutes, I was grateful I had stuck it out, and I recalled that too often I had not pushed myself enough to gain the fullness of such experiences. Toward the end of this interaction, I received a message to come with a camera and count on needing even more perseverance the following day. When I responded, I enjoyed one of my best encounters and took some of my clearest photographs. When I picked these up from the developer, I found that I had captured many wonderful moments that I would not have experienced without my new, more conscious effort to show up for the dolphins.

from overcoming fears to participation

On another day, at the beginning of an encounter, a group of dolphins flanked me on either side. This was rare, but they stayed in that position for quite some time, escorting me directly out to sea. After a while, I became fearful that we were going too far, so I dropped out. As I watched where they were headed, I saw them meet up with another group of dolphins fairly close to where I had stopped. Then a very young, wobbly baby managed a partial jump, showing me what I had missed. I was painfully reminded once again of the importance of showing up for life's abundance rather than allowing fears, pessimism, doubts, or a desire for guaranteed results to block me. When I later looked back at the shore, I noticed that we were not as far out as I had feared, further underscoring the often illusionary quality of anxious concerns that interfere with full participation in life.

choosing comfort over participation

On another occasion, I wanted to pursue the idea of playing the passing game I had started with the dolphin who showed me he could hold a small leaf in his mouth. So I went to the bay the following week with leaves from a maile vine that had been twisted into an open lei. Because no dolphins were in view when I arrived, I left the lei in the water and sent out a message for the dolphins to find it and bring it back to me. Before long, dolphins came into the bay, but none came near me. Finally, disappointed and cold, I decided to get out of the water. The moment I got to shore and pulled my flippers off and my polar suit half down, I had one of the most unusual experiences the dolphins have ever given me.

While I stood at the shoreline with waves lapping at my shins, about thirty dolphins began a dance in single file directly toward me. Each dolphin came within a few yards of me, the closest I have seen them come to the beach, and did one spin in front of me and then made a ninety-degree turn to swim parallel along the shoreline. I received a strong impression that they had the lei, but if I wanted to see it, I would have to get into the water again. This single-file dance looked as though it had been choreographed to Beethoven's "Ode to Joy" and was clearly meant to enchant me. As I stood paralyzed between my desire to see the lei and my desire to get warm and comfortable, the dolphins seemed to be strongly beckoning. I wanted my usual assurance that the dolphins had the lei before I was willing to reenter the water. Thus, I stood there watching for a glimpse of the leaves rather than following my urge to dive into the water and join the dolphins.

My reluctance to show up for this experience reminded me of Ram Dass's story of being on a private bus passing by a special shrine in India and electing to continue on to the hotel for the comfort of a bath and meal rather than stop. After being questioned by others on the bus and reflecting on what kind of a holy man would make such a choice, he directed the driver to turn back and go to the shrine. When they arrived, his guru, whom he had been trying to locate for weeks, was walking along the roadside, and Ram Dass was moved to tears by this fortunate encounter he had almost missed. I realized as I stood transfixed, my wetsuit half on and half off, that I was missing an equally special encounter.

Meanwhile, the dolphins continued to taunt me with their endless parade to the ethereal strains of Beethoven, which rang through my awareness, but unlike Ram Dass, I didn't change my mind—and when the dance was over, I felt a sense of great loss. I can still see the dolphins dancing in my mind and will always wonder if they had the lei with them. But I did learn my lesson. I had let something very precious go, owing to my inability to commit to participation without assurance that the full experience in the form I had ordered would be delivered. I realized that I had done this very thing many times before, and I vowed never to do it again. For the most part, I have kept my vow and since that day have rarely allowed my reluctance to prevail. Whenever I do hesitate, I become alert to this error and quickly correct it. As a result, I now dive more eagerly into full participation in those life experiences I wish to enjoy.

When I realized that my chance to go into the water with the dolphins had passed, I sent them a mental message begging them to continue the game with me at a later date. When I returned the following week, the dolphins were jumping at the shoreline portending their desire to play. Shortly after entering the water, I saw a dolphin swim by with something tan in color that was draped over his dorsal fin. Initially, I was concerned that something was caught on the fin and let him know I would remove it if he would allow me. He very deliberately adjusted it right in front of me so that I could see it was a piece of material he was carrying. Another dolphin paraded a garbage bag draped over his right fin, which he switched to his left side when he reversed direction to come by again. Then he switched it to his tail, which he swished back and forth in front of me. I was stunned. It seemed the dolphins had gotten my message about continuing the leaf game and had shown up with new objects we could use. I was so mesmerized, as I often am in the presence of dolphins, that I forgot to take a picture. Thus, only as they were leaving did I quickly point my camera in the direction of the dolphin with the garbage bag to snap a rather poor shot of his beautiful gift.

I later saw this lesson on the importance of showing up applied with even more powerful results. A dear friend was challenged by a life-threatening illness. She and her husband stayed with us for a week in hopes of seeing the dolphins and receiving some healing energy. We arrived dutifully at the bay for two days in a row and didn't see a single dolphin. I was surprised since I thought the dolphins would love this friend as much as I did and come to help with her healing. The third morning, when I awakened, I received a strong impulse saying that the dolphins would offer a good encounter that day but that my friend needed to learn the lesson of perseverance, which was why they were making her wait. This made sense to me since I too had concerns that my friend might give up rather than win her battle with the illness. When we arrived, we could see that the dolphins had been playing with a group of swimmers, so we got into the water quickly to join them. However, once we were in, the dolphins became scarce.

After staying in the water to support my friend for as long as I could bear the cold, I reluctantly swam for shore. But my friend, who was also cold, elected to stay. Before long, the dolphins began to circle her. Then they disappeared once more. She waited a bit longer, and they circled her again, this time staying longer. Then they left and returned again. I had never seen this friend hang in so long for the full experience, and I was reminded of the message I had received that morning about her need to develop more tenacity in life. Her final encounter after a few hours of waiting consisted of one hundred dolphins swimming with her and her husband for a full hour. It was the best encounter either of these dolphin-lovers had experienced, and my friend learned a good lesson in showing up with perseverance—one that may ultimately have saved her life.

joyful partnership before work

I was feeling pressed for time in meeting my deadline for this book, so I began to push forward with it rather than doing my usual morning program and replenishing activities. One morning in the midst of this period, I felt a call from the dolphins to come to the bay and play. Unfortunately, I felt more compelled to work than to go, even though the call was unusually strong. As a result, I spent the morning putting on my bathing suit, then turning on the computer, then applying sun block, then returning to the computer. Later, I gathered my snorkeling gear together and even headed for the door. Then I returned the gear to the closet and began to type some more. By noon, a strong thought came to me that I had missed the birth of a baby, something I had asked the dolphins to show me. I felt truly regretful that I had not shown up for such a possibility and sensed the dolphins would show me the baby born that day during my next visit.

One day, about a month later, when I went to the bay, the dolphins were there when I arrived and remained there until I left. Yet the only encounter I had that day was a mother and "auntie" presenting a baby about a month old to me, just as I had predicted. It was interesting to me that the dolphins were demonstrating that not even a book on dolphins that might evoke more human interest in preserving their lives should stand in the way of showing up for participating in the play and joy of life. Initially, I was surprised that they seemed to be choosing the joy of life over life itself, but as I learned the rest of their insights, I was able to grasp the profundity of this very dolphin-like choice.

The lesson for me that day was to do a better job of balancing responsibility with play, and I vowed never to allow even important work to hold me back from participating in the joyful part of life's experiences—for what meaning does life have if the dreams and joy are missing? The dolphins had succeeded in penetrating my awareness that *showing up for our dreams* is a critical key to the success and enjoyment of our lives.

life is an "all you can eat"
banquet, but you have to fill your
plate to enjoy it.

CHAPTER 12

the third insight:
focus only on your dreams

Focus only on what you want without distraction in each moment.

When I first heard Wayne Dyer describe his claim of pulling clouds from the sky on a self-help tape, I thought it was a bit pompous. Although I understood the power of intention and physics behind how this worked, I had never thought in terms of average people like myself, or even Wayne Dyer, being able to exercise this ability.

Yet, I had to ask myself why I would not embrace this possibility. Why would I want to manifest good and godly things in this world in hopes of making it a better place, yet insist on feeling helpless and powerless to do so? Thus, I decided one day to practice manifesting clouds as Wayne Dyer had suggested and surprised myself by pulling some white wisps out of a clear blue sky on more than one occasion.

After succeeding in this experiment, I was more in touch with the power of my focused desires, and I could see how I might use it to pull something I truly wanted from the void of our commonly shared universal space called "the Field." Thus, I decided to put this talent to good use by secretly focusing on pulling doubles from the dice while playing backgammon with friends. Once I began to test my skills under these more complex conditions, I was amazed by how often doubles would roll into place on those occasions when my belief in this ability was steady and my focus remained clear.

Then one day, while swimming in the bay at a time when the dolphins weren't there, I decided to see if I could pull them to me out of the clear blue sea in the same way I had pulled the wisps of cloud from the sky and doubles from the dice. The first time I tried this, my focus was undistracted and pure and filled with a novice's faith that the dolphins would show up. And so they did within the next ten minutes. Even though I understood the theory behind this, their arrival was nonetheless startling to me, and I was left with a mixture of euphoria and disbelief in my new reality.

A week later, I had the opportunity to see if I could pull the dolphins to me once again, and, to my surprise, they showed up, although this time they took longer, perhaps because I had introduced feelings of concern about whether or not I could repeat this feat. But even with these successes under my belt, when I floated face down in the water on the morning of my third try, I found myself filled with fears about my ability to repeat my experiment. And sure enough, I failed to pull any dolphins to me. As a result, I began to doubt that their arrival the first two times had been anything more than coincidence. Once this fear clicked into place, I fell prey to old doubts about things not working the way I wanted, which had become a part of my life following a series of traumas I had experienced as an adult.

Suddenly, a strong message came into my mind that sharply interrupted my journey into pessimism. The message reminded me of the importance of *holding my focus only on the things I desire* rather than allowing doubt to creep in and divert my attention.

This clear message was followed by a more detailed explanation of the importance of this idea. During this communication, I was helped to see that quite often, even when our desires are in the being fulfilled, we become impatient over any delay in their delivery and slide into doubt as to whether or not they will arrive. Unfortunately, whenever doubt takes hold in our awareness, it distracts us and interrupts our focus on the dream. Without our focus and the role it plays in pulling the dream toward us, the dream is no longer magnetized to us; it drifts off course and never arrives. Thus, by letting go of our focus on our desires and lapsing into doubt over whether or not we will realize them, we become the ones who abort the fulfillment of our dreams. If we then become discouraged and give up on our other dreams as well, we fail to stay focused on any of them for long enough to give our dreams the time they need to manifest.

This message further revealed that, in addition to doubt, humans are diverted from fulfilling their goals because they allow themselves to get distracted by the habit of focusing on their fears, anger, and judgments instead. They are also sidetracked by such things as gossip, wandering thoughts, and television. And so our actual commitment to focusing on our desires amounts to a smear of peanut butter over a large mound of time spent concentrating on our non-desires as suggested in the film "What the Bleep Do We Know?"

Amazed by the clarity of this insight, I recognized how this had worked in my own life. I had easily focused on my dreams as a child and young woman and had consequently realized most of them. However, the traumas I experienced later in adulthood caused me to lose faith that the truly good things in life would happen to me. Following these events, I had found it more challenging to stay focused on the things I deeply desired or to believe they would materialize. As a result, I was more easily distracted by my problems and the limiting beliefs I had adopted during the period of the traumas. Thus, when there was a delay in the arrival of any of my desires, I would get discouraged and focus on my fear that they would not be delivered.

I also noticed that anytime I shared my dreams with others, I had to then deal with their doubts as well as my own, and this compounded the challenge of staying focused on my goals. I would then put my attention on other distractions, such as why a dream was not materializing, who or what was delaying it, or what deficit in me was blocking its manifestation. Of course every time my focus shifted to not getting something, I would then manifest the very results to which I was now giving my attention—those of not getting my dreams fulfilled.

the power of doubt

Before receiving this insight from the dolphins, I had not realized just how damaging doubt is to the manifestation of our dreams. Yet, after hearing their message, I could see that doubt has the power to abort all movement toward materializing a dream, even when the dream was previously on its way to you and in the process of being fulfilled. This awareness made doubt a far more potent element of failure than I had previously realized.

the positive effect of sustained focus

After absorbing this message, I returned my focus to visualizing the dolphins emerging from the shadows of the sea and swimming playfully toward me. This time, I was able to fight off all the worry and doubt vying for my attention and succeeded in holding my focus on pulling the dolphins to me. Within a few minutes, I heard a dolphin chirp from what seemed like about a mile away, and I realized with satisfaction that the dolphins were on their way to me.

The distance between us offered me a strong visual image of dreams being on their way even when we do not realize they are coming. Clearly, I needed to be more patient and not give up so easily on dreams that have simply not yet arrived. Now, with renewed encouragement and faith, I held my focus on pulling the dolphins to me for another ten minutes. But when they still didn't come, even though I now felt more confident that they would, I again became discouraged and lapsed into doubt.

My skepticism, however, was abruptly interrupted by yet another strong message. This time, I was told that desired things are often on their way but can't be seen and thus guaranteed, even when other indicators, such as the dolphin's chirp, signal that they are in process. As a result, I needed to stay with my focus and faith rather than retreating into doubt, and then shifting to an image of unfulfilled dreams. I was reminded that anytime we fail to stay focused and allow doubt to creep in, whatever is on its way is no longer attracted to us and changes its course. As a result, it will not arrive unless we can restore our faith, rekindle our yearning, and resume our focus on calling it to us.

Accompanying this *verbal* concept impressed in my mind was a clear visual picture that popped into my awareness of the dolphins about a mile away swimming joyfully toward the energy of the yearning within my heart. The image then showed me that if my longing was turned off and replaced with disappointment and doubt, the dolphins would no longer feel pulled to me or attracted by my altered energy and would thus change course and swim elsewhere. This image made it clear that the chirp had signaled that the dolphins were on their way but had not yet arrived and were consequently not yet visible to me. I now realized I would need to sustain my faith in their arrival in order to keep them coming. If I failed to do so, my doubt would interrupt the energy of attraction needed to keep pulling the dolphins to me.

I wondered how often things had been on their way in my life when I had relinquished my focus and lapsed into the repelling energies of doubt, causing what I had wanted to change course and never arrive. I also realized that I had received many signals in life letting me know that good things were on their way, but I had dismissed them, not understanding that these signals were the universe trying to bolster my faith and keep me focused.

Not wanting to lose these dolphins as I had lost other things, I resumed my focus on calling them with the more attractive energies of desire and then seeing them change their course again to swim back in my direction. I now held this picture in place and pulled it to me with the yearning of my heart until at last I could see the forms of the dolphins' bodies emerge from the depths of the blue, swimming joyfully toward me. Following a period of celebratory play together, punctuated by an abundance of clicking and chirping, I emerged from the water dizzy from the experience and sat on the beach awed by the importance of the lesson it contained. Then I realized the dolphins had shown me their third insight for living life effectively. They had reminded me to *focus only on my dreams*.

focus with courage

Before having this experience, I had heard a few people at the bay claim they could call the dolphins and had thought disparagingly, *Oh, sure.* The irony was that, even though I had studied metaphysics for thirty years and fully believed in the unseen power of intention, I still didn't feel comfortable with these claims when made by others.

Then one day, a very bright, psychic woman appeared on the scene and, after announcing that she was going to call the dolphins, went into the bay and began to send out loud toning sounds. Although everyone thought she was a bit eccentric, the dolphins appeared within the next fifteen minutes and were jumping playfully all around her. This woman frequented the bay for the rest of that summer and, for the most part, every time she called the dolphins, they came. Even though I witnessed her success in openly calling the dolphins to her, it never occurred to me that I could do it as well.

In fact, even after I learned to do this, I continued to doubt if it was really happening and lacked the courage to tell others about it. After noticing my cowardice on a day when there were no dolphins in sight, I decided to tell a friend swimming with me that I was going to call them. When I then called the dolphins and they came, both my friend and I were surprised. My friend continues to mention this from time to time, probably because she is still trying to determine, as I am, if it really happened. This is how deeply we have been programmed not to believe in this kind of thing or, even if we do believe in it, to feel afraid of admitting to it.

Yet, as Marianne Williamson points out, the majority of people believe in such phenomena but are afraid to admit it publicly for fear of ridicule. She has often noticed during her speaking tours that if a member of an audience mocks these possibilities, the crowd remains silent. But if two or more people stand up to defend them, the majority will come forth in support of these beliefs. Sadly, many of these silent people include scientists, politicians, businessmen, and others who feel pressured by their peers and professions to hide their true beliefs on this subject even more strongly than do others. They also include religious people who fear that believing such things will betray their religious doctrines, even though many spiritual teachers prompt us to claim our power, and Jesus often told his disciples they could manifest the same kinds of things he demonstrated and more.

Believing in the power of our dreams and the unseen but miraculous way they are manifested is critically important to our keeping them alive and, in so doing, creating a more beautiful humanity and joyful world. If we don't believe in life's invisible ability to deliver our dreams and, thus, lack the courage to desire and focus on them, we move toward hopelessness and despair, enduring our disappointment by enviously watching celebrities and others fulfill their dreams on film and television. Or worse, we numb our pain through depression, drugs, and alcohol or by acting it out with anger and violence toward others. If we can recapture the belief that our dreams can come true and spend time calling them to us, we will awaken to our personal potential and the endless possibilities of our own joyful creations.

focus with strength

Once I understood the effect of focusing, I realized how dangerous a lack of focus had been in my life. I also realized that anytime we lack a strong sense of what we want in life, life won't know what to deliver to us and we will be lost among unformed, inactive, and wispy desires. Thus, I made a concerted effort to heal my general lack of focus on my dreams and convert this weakness to a strength. To do this, I committed to the following program and found that using it creates powerful results in my life. Anytime I let it go, my focus is weakened and my manifestations are less reliable, whereas when I stay with it, remarkable things happen.

steps to strengthen your focus

The following steps can take anywhere from a few moments to several hours. I do them daily in an area of my home set up for meditation. If my schedule is tight, I commit to no less than one hour. However, I prefer to spend even longer at a meditation spot where I can also take a walk. Because this program offers such a fulfilling experience and powerful results, it has become a joyful part of my day instead of a tedious discipline that I must push myself to do. Thus, I spend as much time as I can, but even short doses are helpful. Here, then, are the steps that I use and recommend to others, with individualized selections and adjustments made in time and content to match each person's needs.

SELECT YOUR DREAMS. To keep your dreams fresh and energized, begin each day by making a list of what you want to happen, exactly when you want it to happen, and in precisely what form you want it to manifest for that day and week. Also, on a daily, weekly, or monthly basis, write your goals for the remainder of the month and year and even the next few years. Focusing on your goals during this writing exercise adds energy to them and generates within you a sense of excitement and optimism about realizing them. Moreover, by regularly identifying your dreams and opening yourself to the possibility of their realization, you mobilize your spirit to a happy, hopeful state.

Any time you feel unclear or fuzzy about your dreams, you can use your internal awareness scanner to search through your mental and emotional energy systems or listen within to locate whatever fears you might have about realizing them. This is a helpful step, since the fear of disappointment over unfulfilled dreams can cause us to become afraid of identifying them. It also helps to imagine that you have a magic wand, a fairy godmother, and a benevolent benefactor to provide the resources and skills you might need to manifest even your wildest, most daring dreams. By using these aids to envision yourself free from the fear of failure, your dreams are more likely to surface and be revealed.

Writing while doing this step not only helps you to locate your thoughts and feelings but also allows your dreams to flow easily from within you onto the paper.

JOURNAL THE DETAILS. Once you have selected your dreams, define them in greater detail in your journal. Then identify and write down the steps you will take to accelerate their manifestation. Next, access how you will feel when your dreams have been realized and spend time enjoying this reverie. Writing about your dreams can take the form of a journal entry, a list of goals, a timeline of events, a dream journal, or a letter to your spiritual guides or God. You can also draw pictures of your dreams to put on a visual dream-board. As you draw and write about your dreams, feel yourself claiming them in your heart and at the cellular level deep within you.

CREATE A VISUAL DREAM-BOARD. Because visual dream-boards are such powerful tools, it's helpful to create one filled with pictures, words, and other symbols representing your dreams. Not only do these images and symbols activate a stirring in your heart whenever you focus on them, they bring your dreams to the attention and focus of your powerful subconscious, which will work tirelessly day and night to make them come true. The power of these dream-boards and the conscious and subconscious focus they stimulate were demonstrated to me when I put one together haphazardly and placed it behind my computer.

Six months later, after returning from a trip that I had had no interest in taking, I glanced at my dream-board. What I saw amazed me: A picture of the place I had just visited was attached on my board with an airplane placed overhead. When I looked more carefully at the rest of the board, I realized I had manifested experiences that matched over half of the images posted there. I then removed everything from the board that I did not truly wish to manifest and replaced them with images of my genuine dreams. In the next six months, I manifested all but three of the fifteen dreams on my board and laid groundwork for the remaining three. Now I carefully keep my board updated to reflect my true desires.

ACTIVELY YEARN FOR EACH DREAM. During this step, you can spend time actively calling to you each dream you have identified. Do this by visualizing the event or type of person desired, then actively feel your desire and yearning for that event or person stirring in your heart. Next, visualize this dream moving toward you as your longing for it intensifies. During this period of actively desiring and calling your dream to you, notice how excitement builds within your heart as you and your dream draw closer to each other. Holding your focus on this connection between your heart and the dream for at least sixty seconds is believed to facilitate the fulfillment of your dream.

Throughout this exercise, allow your feelings of longing for the event or type of person desired to grow increasingly stronger within you. This is similar to the feeling of intense love that burns in a person's heart for his or her beloved, or the feeling a child has when he deeply desires the puppy he sees in a pet store window. This energy of desire has the strength to project your feelings of yearning out into the world and onto the event or kind of person desired. By doing this, you pull their arrival into your mind and heart.

In doing this, you influence them to respond in kind. Should your energies be attractive to them, they will feel drawn to you as well, and you will each pull toward the other. By focusing on your longing for your dream in this way, you intensify and strengthen the magnetizing power of your yearning. Once this feeling of excitement has been set in motion, pull the dream all the way out of your future and into your present. This is an important step that prevents your experience of the dream from getting stuck in the future without ever moving toward you to find its way into your present. Then spend time enjoying this experience in your present before ending your visualization.

You can do this step prior to your prayer and meditation time, during your walk or other workout, or at other times throughout the day.

SPEND TIME IN PRAYER. Once you have selected a dream and filled your heart with the fullness of your desire for it, you can spend time in prayer over it. You might begin by getting quiet and expressing your wishes directly to your spiritual helpers and God either through writing or by sending your thoughts to them. To make your prayers feel powerful rather than wistful, you can visualize your guides and God nearby or even in your heart, touching you. Whenever you tune in to their closeness and caring in this way, you will feel encouraged and empowered by the nearness of their loving presence and will no longer feel so alienated, powerless, or lacking in hope. You can begin your prayers with a remembrance and expression of gratitude for their love and the dreams and grace you have already received as well as the ones that are on their way.

Whenever one of your desires is intense and you truly need God's attention, it helps to get on your knees to pray. This will help you feel an immediate connection to God as spirit moves swiftly through you. This usually results in grateful tears, followed by a prayer and an immediate sense from deep within that your prayer has been heard.

It is important to pray with a clear heart attained through forgiving others. And it is valuable to pray regularly for family, friends, and humanity, as well as other species, the world, your guides, and the universe. Not only is this good for them, it stimulates your own heart to open and increases the strength of your manifesting. Similarly, feelings of gratefulness stir the heart and activate this power.

SPEND TIME IN MEDITATION. Following your time in prayer you can slip into a meditation that might last twenty to forty minutes or more. Whenever possible, group prayer and meditation with people who are deeply loved and trusted empowers your efforts in the same way group breathing and swimming empower the lives of the dolphins.

ENJOY FOCUSED BREATHING. Although breath is recommended in most prescriptions for growth and development, like many Westerners, I had always disliked conscious breathing. But after hearing the dolphins gather together in a group to breathe their way rhythmically and consciously into a meditative state, I have changed my attitude. I have also learned from the dolphins how to breathe in a way that is no longer difficult for me.

I now begin with the sense that I can draw a sweet, aromatic fragrance from the air into my body to use with my breath. Flowers, incense, and aroma-therapeutic oils facilitate this imagery. I then strive to smell each essence and, in the process, pull it into me gently through my heart and nasal passages simultaneously. As this fragrant breath slowly finds its way deep into the back of my heart, it stirs the feelings of desire contained there. At times, this desire is simply for God, but it usually includes my dreams as well. Once this breath has completed its caress, I allow it to reverse its course and softly leave through my heart and nasal passage, offering more caresses as it goes.

When this breath is gone, I search for another scent and pull it into me, again taking care to enjoy its fragrance and caressing of my heart. As I take in each breath and release it throughout the day, I periodically remember to allow it to softly wash through the dreams held in my heart, further activating my feelings of desire.

Although there are no annoying instructions to breathe deeply, fill my lungs, or raise my abdomen, I tend to do so naturally in order to pull more of this heavenly essence into my awareness and the back of my heart. After learning to breathe in this manner, the saying that God is no further away than your breath has new meaning for me, and I wonder what role conscious and meditative breathing has played in the evolution of the dolphins.

BLEND BREATH WITH YEARNING. I often combine my new method of breathing with active feelings of yearning and desire. By gently caressing my heart with both breath and yearning in this manner, I am able to experience increasingly higher levels of bliss and joy throughout the day. In doing this, I have gained another glimpse into how the dolphins sustain their consistently joyful state. This has become the most powerful of the steps for me personally, and the more I use it, the greater my joy.

It helps to include music, singing, chanting, toning, and dancing—activities that easily fill our hearts with the kind of vibration, energy, excitement, gratitude, and joy that strengthen the intensity of both our yearning and our attractiveness. Thus, it is helpful to include the sounds of professional chants and music in your morning routine. Or you may wish to produce your own toning and chanting or simply sing a joyful song. Although classical and spiritual music are powerful, playful and popular songs as well as Hawaiian or country music can also help to romance the dream to you. Dancing to these sounds and rhythms adds to the energy and joy of calling the dream into your heart and life. For some, the harmony of group singing or dancing with others enhances not only the power of group meditation and prayer but also the attractiveness of the group.

WALK OR WORK OUT. Following this time for journaling, prayer, and meditation, I go for a daily walk. This provides me with exercise and oxygenation as well as an opportunity to engage in bilateral stimulation believed to help in releasing us from negative emotions and programming us with positive ones. During my walk, I often tap on my heart center while visualizing my dreams. Or, if needed, I tap off negative emotions. Others might prefer a workout or some other form of exercise.

IDENTIFY AND "TAP OFF" NEGATIVE EMOTIONS. Our negative emotions of anger, fear, and pain distract us from our dreams by drawing our energy away from attending to them in favor of focusing on our upset feelings. Consequently, it is important to clear ourselves from the distraction of these emotions as well as the unattractiveness they create in us. To do this, I use my "internal feelings scanner" on my energy system to locate and identify whatever fears, anger, hurt, pain, or other emotional barriers are in the way of my realizing my dreams. As I notice these fear-based and negative emotions, I tap them out of my energy system in accordance with the guidelines for using the "energy therapies" explained in the following chapter.

By removing these disturbed emotions, not only am I released from any emotional barriers to fulfilling my dreams, but also my energies are free to actively focus on my desires. Once these debilitating emotions are released, the confidence I feel as a result of their absence is further strengthened by my bilateral walking and continued tapping.

Once I learned to "tap off" outdated negative emotions, I was free to focus on my dreams, yearn for them with increased energy, and picture myself living joyfully in the midst of them. As a result of this clearing and filling process, endorphins flood through my system, and I begin to feel truly joyful and grateful for dreams already fulfilled as well as the ones I believe are on their way.

REPLACE PERSISTENT ANGER WITH FORGIVENESS. Holding on to feelings of anger and a desire for revenge is synonymous with drinking rat poison and waiting for the rat to die. It not only hurts you more than it hurts the object of your anger, it also whittles away at your attractiveness, health, and happiness, and can even kill your spirit if not your body. Although I have understood this concept for years, there were times when I wasn't ready to let go of some grievance. Or I feared that, if I did let go, I would be condoning some inexcusable act or would not be strong enough to hold my boundaries with the person crossing them. At other times, I was simply too angry to know how to let go.

But each time I have indulged in this delay in releasing my anger, I have paid dearly for it. Thus, no matter how justified anger might be, I have learned to treat it like toxic waste to be released as soon as possible. The "energy therapies" or "tapping" discussed in the following chapter offers a new and powerful way to do this.

CHOOSE HAPPINESS. Over time, I became aware that the dolphins never approached me during times when I was contaminated by feelings of anger, judgment, or unforgivingness and were more likely to draw toward me if I was feeling clear and joyful. Initially, I tried to suppress my unclear feelings in order to attract them, but I soon noticed that, because of their telepathic abilities, my feelings had to be sincere. So rather than continue to hide my negative emotions, I learned to focus only on what I wanted. This had the effect of crowding out thoughts of what I didn't like or want and the unhappy feelings that accompanied those images. Once I committed to focusing only on what I wanted at all times, I found it surprisingly easy to feel happy. I realized in this discovery that the dolphins had taught me how to maintain my attractiveness not only to them but to my dreams through a simple commitment to happiness.

PREPARE THE CONTAINER. In order to fulfill your dreams, God is often required to first prepare the container that will hold them. Since you will serve as the container of your dreams, you are the one who must be prepared to be their holder. To do this, you may need to clear out limiting beliefs, emotions, or patterns of behavior that could prevent you from containing the dream. You may also need to change your circumstances in order to accommodate a larger dream. For example, if you are dreaming of a career change, improved finances, and greater happiness, you might find yourself terminated from a dead-end job, confronted with your limiting beliefs about money, in the middle of a relationship breakup, and forced to move. Although it appears that God has turned against you, these might simply be the ways outdated emotional limitations and lifestyle patterns are being broken apart to prepare you to contain your dreams.

PROTECT PRIVACY. Sharing your dreams with mature family members or prayer partners and close friends sincerely capable of supporting you in fulfilling your dreams adds power to your dreaming. In fact, the dolphins greatly benefit from their cohesive community and are better able to manifest as a result of the group synergy they enjoy. Yet, until humans improve in their ability to care deeply for others and learn to cooperate rather than compete, or until you know people genuinely capable of consistently wanting the best for you, it's best to keep your dreams to yourself. In this way, you will not be required to deal with the doubts, disdain, jealousy, or arguments of others who question your having such dreams or your ability to fulfill them.

CONTINUE UNTIL THE DREAM IS REALIZED. It's important to keep your focusing program going on a daily basis until you have realized your dreams. Remember from the story of the dolphins who were on their way to see me but had not yet arrived that although the fulfillment of your dreams may be delayed, whatever good and godly dreams you have selected that are in alignment with your spiritual journey and higher self will eventually arrive, as long as you are willing to maintain your focus on them and wait for their delivery with patience and faith.

Once I began to incorporate these steps into my life on a daily basis, my focusing skills increased and focusing became a strength for me. This resulted in my dreams being fulfilled more quickly, not always in the order of my preference, but in the order needed to prepare me as a container to hold subsequent dreams.

stay focused with faith versus doubt

There are times, even after we have consistently used the focusing steps, when a dream still isn't manifesting as rapidly as we had hoped. When this happens, we often fall into despair, since we lose not only our faith in the dream but also in God for not listening to our hearts and answering our prayers. We erroneously conclude under these conditions that He does not exist or that, if He does, He doesn't care about us. If we surrender to this despair, we lose all faith in our dreams, in ourselves, and in a friendly universe with a loving God who cares about us at a personal level. Not surprisingly, this leads to feelings of hopelessness followed by depression, and while in this chasm, we lose our focus on our dreams. Whenever this happens, it is our loss of focus, not God's indifference, that causes us to lose the dream.

Thus, anytime dreams are delayed, the thing to remember is that we are still learning how to manifest a good and godly world on this plane. Consequently, rather than turn our dreams over to God to manifest by Himself or give up on the idea that we hold any of the power to help, it is essential during these challenging periods of delay to hold steadily to our focus in order to make our dreams come true.

To successfully sustain our focus during these discouraging periods, we must find a way to keep uncertainty at bay. This can be done most effectively by holding on to our faith in the manifesting process rather than allowing doubt to vie for our attention. Although it's not essential to successful manifestation to believe in God, faith in Him and the goodness of life can accelerate our results. The reason for this, as I understand it, is that while we are on this plane, we are given free will and the opportunity to practice our ability to manifest the lives and world we desire. Yet, whenever we remember to ask for God's help in this endeavor, He will add his power to our budding skills and creations. As for me, I was blessed to have discovered the added power and increased joy of inviting God into my life as a child while fishing from the rocks with my father.

As a young girl growing up in a nonreligious and non-spiritual home, I had been reading *Heidi* and envied her close relationship with God. Because I yearned to believe in Him with the same confidence Heidi had achieved, I decided to make a deal with Him while fishing one day with my dad. My dad had been showing me how to cast a fishing line off the rocks into the rugged Hawaiian shoreline near our home, and when it was my turn to try, I said under my breath to God, "If You exist, I will catch a fish on this throw." My terms were risky, but after reading *Heidi*, I believed God was capable of showing Himself to me in one try. And so, with a deep yearning for God in my heart, I cast my line into the ocean, barely clearing the rocks before me. As I held my breath and slowly reeled in the line, something tugged at it. My dad was certain I had snagged the rocks with my short throw and was shocked to discover that a baby barracuda had managed to attach himself to my bait. As I watched my dad release the fish from the hook and give him back to the sea, my heart began to pound. God had entered this deep place within me as I stood on the rocks in awe of my miracle, watching the baby barracuda swim to freedom. God remained securely in my heart for many happy years following that day, until some painful traumas in adulthood captured my focus, shook my faith, and crowded Him out.

From the time of this experience until the traumas hit, God was clearly with me and so was my faith in the goodness of life. As a result, everything I wanted seemed to manifest, and my life was deeply enriched by an abundance of fulfilled dreams. By contrast, during the years following the traumas when God appeared to be missing, so was my faith in life's grace. Without this faith, as I was now learning, I was missing a critical piece of the manifesting formula for more easily generating good experiences.

I felt grateful when God returned to the edges and shadows of my life a few years after my traumas, but my recaptured "faith" was now tinged with even more doubt than I had experienced as a child. As a result, I constantly asked the universe for evidence, just as I had as a child. But now, I was harder to convince and nagged continuously for more proof. The dolphins had been a big part of the final phase of this proving, and it was no accident that they swam in the same waters where I had plucked the confirming barracuda from the sea so many years before.

Now my book about the dolphins was stirring within me, and my agent was sending the concept to publishers as I flew off to Tonga for a sailing and snorkeling vacation with friends. I decided to make a deal with God similar to the one I had made as a child, and I promised that this would be my last request for proof. I bargained that I would pursue the dolphin book if I was sure the material was true, but I needed one last sign. Thus, I negotiated for God's help in seeing a whale in Tonga as proof that I was in communication with cetaceans. And so, with fear and faith resting side-by-side in my heart, I set off for ten days of sailing at the end of Tonga's whale season with dear friends who had no particular interest in whales.

After a few days in Tonga, we received a report of a friendly calf who had been seen practicing his breaches and spy-hops in the notoriously beautiful Tongan whale nursery. Reports indicated that he and his mother and her escort were the last to leave the area for that season, and he seemed to be making the social rounds. Upon hearing about this calf, I began to call to him with my heart during meditation and felt him respond with a desire to see me as well. The connection I had with him felt surprisingly mutual and reminded me of St. Francis of Assisi's saying, "What you yearn for also yearns for you." This was the first time I could actually feel the yearning of the thing yearned for prior to our first encounter, and it felt wonderful. These moments of mutual yearning between us evoked a deep knowing in me that we would meet, accompanied by an image of the calf breaching off the bow of our boat.

A few days later, when we heard that this friendly calf had visited with people on another boat, a pang of jealousy hit me, followed by a moment's fear that he would fail to greet me as well. However, because of my meditations and focusing time, these fears

146

were happily fleeting and were replaced by my faith that he would, in fact, visit me sometime before we left.

Next, we were told during dinner at the Hunga Bay Restaurant that a boy snorkeling outside the bay the previous day had heard a loud chirp in the water. When the boy looked in the direction of the sound, he saw this friendly calf looking back at him, and they gazed at each other until the whale's mother arrived to squire her little socialite away.

Because we were told that the last sighting of this calf had been to the right of Hunga Bay as you leave, I asked our captain if we could take that route. He gently explained that because it would take us completely off course, it wasn't a viable option. Since it was our last day, I felt disappointed but not fully discouraged. By staying focused on what I wanted and continuing to use the dolphins' tools for manifestation, I managed to hang on to my faith in spite of the conditions. That night as I prepared for bed, I meditated on the calf and could feel his presence in my heart once again. Thus, in spite of the poor odds for success, my faith in seeing this friendly calf deepened as I dropped off to sleep, caressing my heart with this desire.

The following morning, with our sailboat exiting as planned to the left of the bay, I looked longingly to the right, and I immediately saw a small white puff. It was a baby whale spout several hundred yards in the distance, and my heart began to pound. When I told our captain about it, he sweetly agreed to turn our boat to the right and headed slowly and carefully in the direction of the spout. We were halfway to where the blow had been when the calf startled me into a holler with a full-bodied breach about twenty feet from the bow where I was sitting. He surfaced shortly thereafter with his mother, and they dove together under our boat and surfaced again on the other side, where they joined their escort and swam out in front of us lazily along the surface as we followed along a good distance behind.

Not only was I thrilled by how well the dolphins' lessons worked when I used them, but God had delivered once again—this time a whale rather than a barracuda, and with it, my faith had been fully restored. The thing I realized this time that I had failed to notice as a child was that faith is something you must keep in place, even when the evidence is scanty or lacking or has simply not yet arrived. This is why it is called faith, and learning to hold on to it in the middle of life's journey is the work of adulthood and an important key to successful manifestation.

I would keep my end of the bargain and complete the book. And I would hang on to my faith in God this time, with or without evidence, as well as my faith in manifesting my dreams.

you can manifest your dreams
by holding them in the fire of your
heart, kept brighter with faith.

CHAPTER 13

the fourth insight:
be attractive to your dreams

Entice the dream to you as you would entice your beloved.

If we are to draw the things we have selected as goals and now wish to call them to us, we must learn how to be attractive to the dream in the same way we strive to be attractive to a lover whose attention we desire. I first awakened to the importance of this concept when the dolphins delayed their initial contact with me until I could make myself more attractive to them. But it wasn't until they later repeated this idea that I realized that it was the fourth of the dolphins' insights for how we can manifest our dreams.

This insight was reintroduced during a time when I was filled with anger over the commercialization of the dolphin experience and the busloads of visitors overpopulating the bay. My irritation was fueled by the insensitive way this surplus of swimmers chased after the dolphins, often cutting in front of others to get closer to them.

One day when I was feeling particularly annoyed by these people, my guide dolphin circled me several times with his eyes closed.

Then a message was impressed in my mind that the dolphins could handle the visitors and didn't need my help. I was further assured that having people come to the bay, even if there were too many of them or they lacked good manners, gave the dolphins an opportunity to work with people and help to raise their level of consciousness. Only by having this opportunity would they be able to influence our species to be more caring of the planet and its inhabitants. Consequently, the dolphins did not want additional laws that would prevent their interactions with people other than the non-harassment regulations already in place. Nor did they want people like me to feel angry on their behalf since the anger only added further to the negative energies of the world.

This was the closest I had come to being scolded by the dolphins, and I later learned that the largest group in the water that day consisted of Japanese visitors belonging to an organization to promote the protection of dolphins and whales in Japan, a country that still kills and eats cetaceans.

On another occasion, after I had succeeded in releasing one of my judgments, the dolphins gathered around me in a serious, silent mood. The message I received let me know that my urge to care about the dolphins was of value both to me and to the planet. But the part of me that got upset with the behaviors of others, condemned them, and then felt superior and separate from them, was of no use to me or the dolphins. It not only sullied my heart with anger but sent negative energies into their bay and world. These energies worked more against the goals of the dolphins and were far less attractive to them than the poor manners of the naive swimmers chasing after them. This concept was reinforced by the photos of the water crystals in Dr. Masaru Emoto's book, so clearly showing the impact of my anger on the bay's water. (These can also be seen in the water crystal cards published by Council Oak Books.)

I was further sent the message that if I would observe the dolphins, they would offer me a model for handling difficult situations with greater equanimity. I would see, for example, that they often teased some of the chasers in order to wear them out, while ignoring others altogether. In short, they would handle these people individually according to their particular needs, just as they had done with me on so many occasions—but they would always do it without anger.

I was reminded of the many times the dolphins had telepathically tuned in to my ex-husband's and my quarrels as well as our negative thoughts and responded by stopping all chatter, sometimes impressing me with their hurt or surprise at my judgments, and then leaving the area. In this way, they taught me that anytime someone's energies are negative, I could simply move away, while remaining loving.

I was further shown that I can go back later if I am so inclined, as the dolphins often do, and give people another chance. Or, if I am not ready, I can remain loving from a distance. I was also taught that as I learn to hold to this more benign response, the conscience of persons who have transgressed will eventually reveal to them the things they are doing that are in error and not working well. In the meantime, it is not my job to derail my own good heart in order to act as the personality police. My only job is to keep love flowing from my heart at all times no matter how others behave. In this way, I am free to fulfill my mission of sending only good intentions into the world while feeling loving and connected to others.

Following this message, I noticed a dolphin playfully teasing an aggressive swimmer right in front of me by coming back to him repeatedly after short dashes of escape from his grasp. Since this was not the dolphins' usual response to chasing, I assumed this gesture of playfulness with the aggressive swimmer was for my benefit, because I was being strenuously ignored that day, as always happens whenever my irritations get the best of me. The moment I understood the dolphins' message about my anger, the playful dolphin below me eyed me as a quarterback might eye his receiver and released a large bubble from a distance that was perfectly coordinated with my speed of motion. As the bubble traveled slowly upward at a perfect angle toward me, I reached out to carefully grasp it in my hands. I had seen a video of two young dolphins playing volleyball with one of these viscous and stable bubbles that rise slowly and don't pop immediately, and I hoped I could bounce this one back to the dolphin who had blown it.

However, just as I reached for it, one of the chasers swam quickly in front of me and stuck his finger into the bubble, causing it to abruptly pop. This was the first bubble I had seen the wild dolphins blow, and after watching the man pop it, I was sorely challenged to hold on to the message about calming my anger. But, in the middle of my struggle, I was gently reminded once again to send love, not anger, into the ocean, if nothing more than for the sake of the dolphins. I was also promised that I would receive many more bubbles, so I could let that one go rather than allow it to cause me to become so unattractive.

That day, I began to grasp just how much anger discharges negative energies into the world even when it's based in righteousness. Anger is not only unattractive but pervasively hurtful to everyone and everything in its path, including myself. I was reminded of the images of crystallized water that had been sent good energies juxtaposed with the images of water that had been bombarded with negative energies. It explained why every great teacher from previous centuries has taught that love is the only valid approach to absolutely everything, and it became clear in a new and vivid way that if we each succeeded in following this one lesson, only love would prevail on the planet. For the first time, I truly understood the potential outcome of "turning the other cheek" as the dolphins do. In fact, their ability to consistently do this added to my growing perception that they had developed in a higher, more evolved manner than their human counterparts.

I also realized that if I could succeed in copying the dolphins' ability to remain loving under all circumstances, I would not only be attractive to my dreams but would also fulfill my true purpose of letting only love flow through me at all times. If all of us would harness our intention to consistently send love instead of the negative energies we have grown so used to sending, we could rather easily bring heaven to earth. Although we have heard this message before, we seem to think it's beyond our reach and don't really try to achieve it. Yet, not only do the dolphins succeed in realizing this goal a few miles from our shores, they also make it look both easy and fun.

I finally realized, too, that this was my first introduction to the concept of kenosis, or the emptying ourselves of the various "positions" over which we spend our lives fighting, so as to allow love and God to fill the emptiness. I could also see that if we could ever manage to use this concept in its broader context as Templeton Prize-winner George Ellis and others suggest, we would have an entirely new, more powerful, loving, and joyful experience.

removing the barriers to attractiveness

Although the goal was now clear, determining how to remove the barriers to my attractiveness remained a challenge. Indeed, maintaining my appeal to my dreams following my earlier adulthood traumas had been the hardest part for me. To succeed, I had to figure out how to heal the various injuries the traumas had inflicted, tame the fear I had adopted about my ability to draw good things to me, and release the anger that had crept into my heart during that difficult period. I realized too that I was not alone in this struggle. As a counselor for thirty years, I had come to understand that all of the fears, problems, and limits people accumulate in the course of their lives are reactions to unhealed traumas they have encountered along the way.

The answer to how I and others might heal and release these outdated wounds came to me in the early 1990s, when I was introduced to the new, yet dramatically effective, "energy therapies."

the "energy therapies"

Powerful "energy therapies," often referred to simply as "tapping," are currently surfacing in the field of therapy and operate in a manner similar to the way the dolphins achieve their healing and happiness. These therapies have the potential to rapidly release energy we carry from past traumas and the accompanying fear, hurt, and pain that were too overwhelming for us to process and release at the time of the initial trauma. These unresolved traumas were subsequently converted to energy in the form of emotional pain and then stored in our bodies' energy systems. There, they serve as outdated emotional baggage we carry into our lives. Whenever these stored energies are re-stimulated by a similar event in the present, our emotions become overly responsive or "accessed." And when this happens, we become defensive and angry or withdrawn, as we did when we were younger and felt helpless in the face of these kinds of events.

Because of this cycle, each unresolved issue from the past, now stored as an outdated yet debilitating energy within us, serves as a barrier and distraction to the forward movement of our lives. Thus, finding a way to release these energies is critical to our ability to return to the natural state of freedom, courage, self-confidence, and joy that we experienced prior to the traumatic events, going all the way back to our earliest childhood traumas.

In the past, these pockets of anger, hurt, pain, and fear remained trapped in our energy systems for years, if not the rest of our lives. But now, with the discovery of the energy therapies, these outdated and toxic emotional energies can be rapidly released by tapping on the end points or meridians of our energy systems (as used in acupuncture), while we are in touch with the disruptive feelings. By doing this, we free ourselves from these emotional barriers to our positive choices and happiness.

Interestingly, this tapping not only feels remarkably similar to the tapping the dolphins send to us with their sonar pings, which can often be felt on our skin, but the results are surprisingly comparable in speed and effectiveness. Because of this similarity in sensation and results, it makes sense that sonar tapping would be one of the ways the dolphins provide us with the release of outdated emotional and physical energies, leaving us with the commonly reported feelings of renewal and well-being following our time with them.

The result of tapping is similar to and feels much like deleting an unwanted program from our system, leaving us feeling a great deal clearer and free of that particular negative energy. Over time, we can tap to release all of the places in us that hold the old fearful, hurt, and anger, as well as the muddled approaches we have used to alleviate these feelings such as withdrawal, competitiveness, compulsions, deceit, and manipulation. Once this housecleaning is done, only the clear, higher self remains, which is felt and expressed as our natural state of pure love and playful joy.

(For more information on how to utilize these techniques, see my website at www.bobbiesandoz.com.)

establishing force fields of harmony and love

The value of releasing outdated traumatic energies, either as a result of human tapping or sonar pinging from the dolphins, is that it allows us to unload whatever negative energies we still carry from the past that trigger current feelings of fear, hurt, and pain. When these old feelings are triggered, as they often are by current events that remind us of them, they influence the way we feel and the choices we make.

For example, if an old fear of failure is triggered in me by some new opportunity that stimulates my memory of a past failure, I may behave in a withdrawn manner to avoid the fear welling up in me. Thus, rather than pursuing the new opportunity, I may counter my own good by avoiding it. Or I might choose defensiveness and anger to ward off the uncomfortable feelings and strike out at the people offering me the opportunity or friends encouraging me to pursue it. Because this fear from the past, now stored in my energy system, serves as the force behind these emotional responses and sabotaging choices, it blocks me from realizing my full potential. Thus, only when I am free of this outdated fear am I truly free to select clearer, more effective responses in the present.

Whenever a choice is made, whether as a reaction to old fears or from a place of clarity and freedom, we will tend to repeat that choice in the future until it becomes a pattern in our lives. Once in place, this pattern will continue to be copied and repeated by us and others. Thus, if we decide to be positive, we not only draw positive experiences to ourselves in a repeating pattern but also influence others to do the same. This choice and the repeating pattern it creates becomes a template to which future choices will conform.

As a result of this inclination to repeat our choices, our initial choices often lead to familiar patterns of behavior, even when they are destructive. These templates then build on themselves and serve as guidelines into which individual and societal behaviors and beliefs are molded. This explains why a society such as ours can have a period of increasing violence that becomes a challenge to interrupt. And it demonstrates the importance of being released from the negative emotions that drive our unclear and destructive choices.

Fortunately the dolphins and the energy therapies are showing us a way to rapidly achieve the relief we seek. Once we are released from these interruptive energies and their templates, we are free to select new, more effective templates upon which to build better lives. When others join us in making these more positive choices, we become united in creating an even stronger force field of beneficial energies in our world.

Dolphins continuously tap each other with sonar, which regularly discharges any negative energies they might have. This, in turn, enables them to remain consistently clear in their energies and selection of positive choices. As a result, they are not only filled with the loving and harmonious energies of the higher self but band together to create a powerfully positive vortex into which additional positive energies are drawn. In this way, dolphins create a compelling force field of good within themselves, which sends its own goodness out into the world while drawing more goodness back to itself. Baby dolphins born into this force field are swept up in it and begin their lives with positive templates.

By contrast, humans are born into a world filled with a number of templates that simply don't work—based on the traumas of inadequate parenting, a weak school system, and an excess of violent images. As a result, we have had more trouble holding loving energies in our hearts, focusing on our positive dreams, and uniting to create a force field of good that could draw more goodness to us and our world. Instead, we have been seduced by the fear and pain of past traumas, feelings of separateness, and the anger, greed, and judgment these emotions stimulate in us.

Because we have been living in a society that inflicts so much hurt and pain on its inhabitants, most of us are at risk for developing expectations—and matching receptors—that will draw more hurt and pain to us. Moreover, in response to our own pain, we may participate in hurting children and others and further fuel this cycle of human pain.

Clearly, the discovery of the energy therapies as a way to effectively release these traumas is critical to interrupting this unfortunate cycle at an accelerated rate. Once this is accomplished, we will be free to develop and expand our loving and joyful feelings and the matching receptors shaped to draw more love and joy into our lives and world.

the dolphins as "energy therapists"

I was blessed to have become involved with the energy therapies in the early stages of this movement and to use them to release many of the outdated negative energies I had accumulated within my own energy system. Then one day, after I used the energy therapies to tap off a parcel of these fearful energies, the dolphins were particularly attentive. Not only could I feel their sonar actively pinging my skin, but they also performed three of their spinning helix braids under me. These were accompanied by a confirming message that one aspect of their healing work is that they do, in fact, tap on us with their sonar to help release blocked energies in our physical, emotional, and spiritual bodies.

Following this encounter, I felt even freer of the negative energies I had been releasing and wondered if the dolphins' sonar and spins had accelerated the process. In addition, the joy I felt after my swim with the dolphins that day was even more intense than usual, and the dolphins impressed a second message, showing that their tapping away our negative energies was part of why people feel so healed and clear after swimming with them. Realizing the dolphins also use tapping to help keep us clear and protect our attractiveness helped me to value the energy therapies even more. I vowed to write a user-friendly book on it for children and adults to make this simple technique simpler and available for everyone to use in their daily lives as the dolphins do. Once people understand how to use this simple tool, they will have at their fingertips the power to keep themselves and their children clear of the traumas that feed our fears and block our success and to make room for a surge of positive energies that better serve our confidence, success, and joy.

practicing attractiveness

The importance of practicing our attractiveness at all times was underscored during a whale-watching workshop I attended on the Big Island of Hawaii. The leader had set the date quite late in the season, and, although we were having some wonderful dolphin encounters, whale sightings had been sparse. Many members of our group had flown thousands of miles for this experience, and people were becoming tense.

On our day off, my friend and I drove to the north end of the island where whales preparing to return to Alaska would be spending their last days. To our surprise, we had failed to see a single whale during our hour-long drive to this spot or during the second hour, when we sat on a wall overlooking the waters they were known to frequent. Lingering there for a few more moments before going to lunch, we pondered why the leader had scheduled the workshop so late in the season. Following that question, a thought was impressed on my mind that it was not a matter of the season or the number of whales remaining but a matter of our consciousness as to whether or not we would see them. As I shared this thought with my friend, a whale rose full-bodied out of the water on the horizon, followed by another whale imitating the first breach. To our sheer delight, these two whales then proceeded to jump and play for the next half hour and then followed us along the coastline as we drove to lunch.

The following day, a woman who had a great energy joined us. She didn't seem to have the same fear the others carried that we would not see dolphins or whales. Perhaps her confidence came from the fact that she also had with her a drum, which cetaceans are known to enjoy. While she drummed, the group began to relax and unite through the rhythm of her beat. As we loosened up and joined in with our own movements and sounds, whales began to present themselves. Some did body or tail breaches while others waved their pectorals from a distance.

Before long, a female appeared very close to us. She spy-hopped to check us out and then circled around our boat. Next, she rolled over on her back very close to the surface, creating a beautiful palette of pale blue as her white belly mixed with the cobalt hues of the ocean. She glided rapidly toward the boat in this position as we stared in wonder as to what she had in mind. She kept coming at a steady pace, looking as though she would hit the boat, while we held our breath and waited. Without slowing down, she slipped easily under the boat, where she remained for a few minutes before sliding out again at the bow. Everyone was blown away. Some became instantly nauseated and felt as though they had been zapped by an energy rendering them initially toxic, then healed. Others were ebullient and lost in joy. And still others were stunned into silence.

Once tension and fear were out of the way and we had become an attractive and playful group, we were able to draw the kind of experiences to us we had yearned to have when we embarked on this adventure. A month later, I was given an opportunity to practice this lesson on the importance of maintaining our attractiveness under considerably more challenging conditions.

It took place at a week-long workshop for swimmers new to the dolphin experience, which I attended to be with a dear friend I had not seen in years. I was surprised by the insensitive behavior of the leaders as they over-swam their guests and dove in front of them into the dolphin groups, consistently scaring them away. They would then surface to proclaim that the dolphins were letting them swim in the middle of the pod. The beginners were taken in by these claims, but I was distressed by how often the leaders were spoiling good dolphin encounters for their workshop participants. In the past, I would have allowed my irritation with this situation to destroy my own positive energies and attractiveness. But now, I was aware that any anger I entertained and allowed to take root in my heart would not only render me unattractive but would also repel the dolphins and other positive experiences from coming to me and possibly the entire group. As a result, I spent much of that week in prayer and meditation, calling gentle and loving feelings to rest in my heart.

The last day of the workshop was glorious from beginning to end. As sunlight danced on the blue and green water, whales began to entertain us with full-bodied leaps into the air. I marveled at their seeming defiance of the laws of physics and wondered at their ability to repeatedly raise their up to fifty-ton bodies as high as fifty feet out of the ocean with the help of only a single tail and a pair of spindly fins.

When we later arrived at one of the inlets along the shore, it was filled with about eighty dolphins playing with a small group of gentle and attractive swimmers from another boat. We pulled alongside them and got into the water where we could see the dolphins beneath us. But once again, our leaders warded them off with direct approaches and dives rather than remaining on a parallel course or offering enough space for the dolphins to approach only if desired. I was grateful that there were enough dolphins for everyone to enjoy a peek at them but regretted that the extended encounters were being interrupted. It wasn't long before the dolphins left, and we were instructed to return to the boat in order to follow them.

As I was swimming toward the boat and feeling uncomfortable about the plan to pursue the dolphins, I came across the captain, who had spotted two rays and had his video camera in tow. I followed along behind, and when I saw the rays, I began to call them silently from my heart. I was startled by their ninety-degree turn to swim directly toward me and felt grateful that I had meditated myself into a loving state. The captain was also pleased and pointed his camera at them with excitement. But our reverie was soon broken when one of the workshop leaders emerged. He physically bumped into my body as he rushed over me toward the rays, who now did another ninety-degree turn away from us as they dove and swam to safety. I too did a ninety-degree turn and headed for the boat, working hard to quell my rising irritation.

There I ran into Peri, a delightfully loving young woman who runs a meditation center. She calmly invited me to slip off with her to greet some dolphins who were approaching from the other side of our boat. I joined her, and we began to tone in unison into the water as we held hands and called the dolphins to us with our hearts. We were soon surrounded by about twenty dolphins who paraded in front of us for the next ten to fifteen minutes. We cooed as they swam by us in twos and threes, gazing, smiling, caressing each other, and holding "fins." An adorable wrinkly baby repeatedly showed off his brand-new jumping skills as we cheered him on with squeals of delight. I knew that babies jump about two hours after birth and calculated that these were probably his first attempts. It was an honor that his mother had let him come so close to us for his debut.

Next, three adults approached and engaged us in gazes and blasts of loving energy, prompting Peri to comment that it felt as though she was receiving *darshan,* or the grace of the guru. Then the mother and baby came by again; this time the baby was attached to the mother for nursing.

Eventually my friend Sue and others arrived. Sue and Peri and I held hands as the three dolphins continued to make passes at us for the next few minutes. I felt blessed that I had enjoyed this experience with the beautiful Peri and that my friend Sue and the others had shared briefly in it as well. I was also pleased that I had succeeded in remaining peaceful and realized that doing so had protected our special experience. Moreover, when we returned to the boat, I noticed a shift had taken place within me, and I was able to feel genuinely loving toward the leaders. As a result of holding on to love, not only had I succeeded in being attractive to my dreams, but I was also healing my heart.

It became apparent that this was the goal for humanity—to feel this level of peacefulness and love in each other's presence no matter what conditions challenge us, to allow our hearts to open and welcome others no matter how they behave, to assume the best from them as we do the dolphins, to give them the best of ourselves as the dolphins do, and to send ripples of love and caring to everyone under all circumstances.

This would create more attractive receptors for us all, which would, in turn, draw abundantly more good fortune from the universe to humanity.

what you yearn for also yearns for you.
—St. Francis of Assisi

CHAPTER 14

the fifth insight:

play while you wait for your dreams to arrive

Hold the faith that your dreams are on the way, then be happy while you wait for them to arrive.

Nothing is worse than to select a dream and then to feel miserable simply because it has not yet arrived. Thus, just as we must wait calmly for our restaurant orders to be prepared and served, whenever a goal in life has been identified and called for, we must learn to wait patiently for it to arrive.

Yet, although restaurant orders will be filled fairly promptly no matter how we behave, we must find something to do while we wait for our unpredictable orders from life to arrive—particularly when a request may take some time to be fulfilled. We must also find a way during this waiting period to remain attractive to the dream or it will no longer feel drawn to us, which will in turn prompt it to change its course and never show up.

To remain attractive to our dreams while we await their delivery, the dolphins teach us to *play while we wait*. Not only does this fifth insight give us something joyful to do, but it also assures our continued attractiveness and joy as we wait. It also teaches us not to delay engaging in the fun of life while waiting for our goals to be met, because such delay trains us to use play as a reward rather than as an integral and important part of life to enjoy—without reason—as the dolphins do.

Thus, rather than succumb to the repelling attitudes of impatience or disappointment while waiting for the dream's arrival, we can protect our attractiveness by opting to relax and play. This happier, more relaxed state also encourages loving and joyful receptors to form which then draw and hook us up with the essence of the loving and joyful experiences we desire.

The dolphins often train us to increase our patience by first making us wait and then engaging us in teasing and play. This teaches us to allow the waiting period to be more relaxed and joyful rather than so intense or as fodder for our anxieties. Interestingly, a similarity to the dolphins' approach was noted in the Princeton University PEAR experiments (see pgs. 119-120), in which the most relaxed and playful operators were the ones who achieved the greatest success in influencing randomly programmed machines to respond to their requests. By contrast, the operators who were anxious or who "tried hard" introduced tense rather than attractive energies to the experience and had the least success.

the essence of play

Play can take any form that brings us relaxation, fun, and joy. For example, in the PEAR experiments, the operator who had the greatest success would make her selections for the machine and then eat vanilla yogurt and read while she waited. Although eating and reading worked for her, others might prefer to do things that will put them more consciously into a focused yet relaxed and happy state, such as meditating, singing, playing an instrument, or dancing. These particular kinds of activities help to keep a person's yearning energized and active during this period of play, which is helpful to anyone like myself who possesses a less natural strength of desire or intensity of focus.

Others do better by forgetting all about their goals and shifting to a new activity such as taking a shower or bath, running, swimming or working out, walking, playing a game, or daydreaming. Still others become most relaxed and joyful by immersing themselves in nature or sitting in the sun. The key is for people to do whatever will help them to feel the most relaxed, happy, and playful.

relax, but don't surrender

Although the dolphins suggest that we learn to relax and play while we wait for our dreams to arrive, they also caution us to do this without surrendering the dream or our continued excitement about it.

I initially thought the message to "relax" and "play while we wait" was similar to the one taught in other manifestation programs that encourage people to "let go" and "release" the dream or "surrender" it to God. However, the dolphins repeatedly let me know that this is not what they mean and that release and surrender can be confused with a feeling of "giving up" or "abandoning" the dream. Instead, they are suggesting that we hold our dreams actively in our hearts while turning our attention to humor and play as we wait for them to arrive. The dolphins revealed how this fifth insight works in the following way.

I drove out to the bay at a time when I felt discouraged as a writer and ready to "let go of my dream" to publish a series of books. Perhaps, I thought, I would just retire instead to a golf and tennis community where I could enjoy more relaxation and play while engaging in prayers and meditation as my contribution to the world. In part, this was a sulky thought and a threat to God that I was ready to drop out of viewing life as purposeful unless He would help me out more. But it was also a genuinely attractive alternative to the agony and ecstasy of authorship, and my threat was not idle.

The dolphins had not spent much time playing with people in the bay that year, and news of this change was spreading. Consequently, the beach was considerably less crowded than it had been for quite some time. But now, the dolphins were beginning to offer periodic visits again, and I decided to go to the bay in hopes of being chosen for one of these more rare encounters.

When I arrived, a group of swimmers had just finished playing with the dolphins and were getting out of the water. Thus, I was not sure the dolphins would stay longer for my swim, but I decided to jump in the ocean anyway. Although a dolphin established voice contact with me the moment I submerged my head, the pod remained down the beach from where I was swimming. I felt let down but was pleased with the gracious way I was handling this rejection and decided to surrender to the reality that I was not being selected for a swim. Just as I had this thought, I received a message that surrender was not the answer, because if I surrendered the dolphins would no longer be drawn to the energy of my yearning. Yet, it was also important that I not become filled with the unattractive energies of fear or attachment as a result of my concerns about not realizing my dream.

Although I grasped the truth of this, I was unclear about how to accomplish such a delicate balance between submitting to relaxation and remaining attractive without giving up the dream or becoming anxious about its not manifesting. But soon, a strong message came through that I could simply "play while I waited." This would keep my order from the dolphins active and alive while I enjoyed myself and maintained my attractiveness to them. In short, playing while I waited would naturally and easily put me into the desired state of balance, whereas trying to get there by "letting go" or "surrendering" the dream would have the opposite effect.

Since this message was so different from most spiritual prescriptions suggesting that dreams be released and turned over to God, the dolphins repeated it several times. They further expressed that, since it was my dream, I should not abandon the project and expect God to handle it on His own. He was willing to help, if asked, but would not take it over while I "let it go" in order to "turn it over to God" to finish. Although it was a team effort, it had been my dream, and I needed to stay in the game in order to help create it and strengthen my manifesting skills.

The idea continued with a concept very new to me, but one that made sense. Humanity has always tried to sidestep the fact that we have been given free will and are meant to co-create on this plane. We always want to give this away to heroes and masters as well as to God. Then when it doesn't go well, we like to blame it on God and fail to realize that the manifestations in our world are the result of our dreams and focus, not God's. The message continued that humanity's purpose is to be an active part of what happens here on this plane and to act as an instrument of bringing heaven to earth. In view of this, humans need to realize that God does not require practice with manifesting dreams, since He is able to bring all of our dreams into full realization in a moment. By contrast, we are the ones who need the practice, and involving ourselves in the process of manifestation is part of our purpose and mission. Thus, our job is to keep our dreams actively alive in our hearts, our faith in them steady, and to simply "play while we wait" in order to enhance our attractiveness to the things being called.

Once I absorbed this message and began to relax into my enjoyment of cooing to the fish while keeping vital my desire to swim with the dolphins, the dolphins appeared. My three closest dolphin friends swam straight toward me so directly I thought they might hit me. The moment I considered this possibility they pulled out, then circled around, and next swam straight toward me again. Because this action was so uncharacteristic, I felt afraid, but a message revealed that they were acting especially frisky in the spirit of "playing while you wait." Next, these dolphins joined several others swimming at a slower tempo under me. Then they left.

It was a short visit that felt somewhat aborted, but I elected to surrender graciously to accepting this brief encounter. Again, I was chided for not learning the lesson I had just been taught and was told to hold my focus on what I really wanted—and so I did. This time, the dolphins took longer to return, but I managed while waiting to hold both my desire and a sense of playfulness in my heart.

Eventually, they showed up for another encounter in which about thirty dolphins played with me for an hour or more. During this time they showed me a number of new experiences, some reflecting answers to questions I had formed before coming. For example, in response to my query about how many dolphins joined together to form the spinning helix braid, a group of large dolphins gathered carefully under me and got into position to do the spin. They remained in that position while I counted how many there were. Just as I realized I was having trouble counting them, they broke apart and got into formation again, staying motionless while I more easily recounted them. Then they enacted the spinning braid in slow motion as if it was a demonstration in response to my questions about just how they did it. I even managed to get some photos in focus of this normally fast-moving activity.

Next, a group of five mothers came by with their young babies and circled me several times while each baby pulled away from his mother for a solo moment with me. One blew a bubble, another squealed, another swam upside down, and another did a partial jump. Following this debut, a mother about ready to give birth and her two escorts came very close, circled me multiple times for the next half hour, and then emitted her pre-birth dark-colored liquid before leaving. Next, four pregnant mothers arrived and circled me several times. It occurred to me that this was significant in some way, and I wondered if I might be given a chance to witness one of these births. A week later, I learned that my own first grandchild had been conceived, so perhaps this abundance of pregnant mothers and babies was a prelude to our family's happy event.

Every time I thought my experience was complete, more dolphins came by, some in pairs and threes, all moving in close to say "Hi." When this blessing came to an end an hour later, I swam to shore filled with deep gratitude. Now I was genuinely satisfied and ready to say good-bye rather than "surrender" something I still desired. I was also satisfied with the dolphins' lesson reminding me not to fall into the powerless feelings that often accompany "letting go" under the guise of "spiritual surrender" to the notion "it was not meant to be," rather than facing the reality of an unfulfilled dream.

Instead of the release and surrender I had practiced without success for so many years, I was now learning to energize the call of my dreams to me by holding my focus more vigorously on them. Yet, even though my yearning was still active rather than passive as a result of "letting go," I had found a new way to remain attractive while waiting for the dream to arrive. The key was to keep my focus and yearning active in my heart as I played while I waited for my dreams to arrive.

Once the joy of play filled my actively yearning and happy heart, I could see how I would become a magnet to all of the dreams I wished to draw to me. In short, my heart would be filled with desire as well as loving, joyful receptors shaped to draw equal measures of magic to my life. After experiencing how this felt, I could see how the dolphins regularly engage in the same kind of joyful, attractive energy they were teaching me to hold. I also noticed that whenever I used this heart-stirring step, my own manifestations were realized faster.

Anytime we engage in desire mixed with joyful play in harmony with others, as the dolphins do in their constellations of two or more, the magnified energy of our combined bliss, gratitude, and grace will generate even more vitality to our dreams and draw greater goodness to our lives. Whenever I have encountered superpods of dolphins aligned in similar kinds of positive energy, the power and joy are giddily contagious.

using the dolphins' first five insights to manifest my dreams

The dolphins had taught me five of their six principles of manifestation, and I was ready to practice applying them to my daily living. To my surprise and delight, not only were these steps easy to follow, my results were better than I had anticipated.

summary of the insights

As I began to weave the dolphins' lessons into my life, I became more aware of how often my dreams had not been clearly defined in the past. I also noticed the weakness of my attention and focus on them and how often my thoughts turned instead to my problems or doubts whenever one of my dreams was delayed. Now I was learning to hold on to my feelings of desire and yearning while remaining attractive to my dreams by playing while I waited for them to arrive.

As a result of this shift, things seemed to fall more easily into place. Good health, clients, money, special experiences, fortunate connections, and a greater sense of ease and joy were taking root in my life. I began to realize from my own results that sharing these insights with humanity was the dolphins' real purpose in talking to me and that they would be helpful to all people wanting to create richer, fuller lives for themselves and a better world for us all.

Although all of this was wonderful, I had recently identified a number of more challenging dreams I wanted to realize in a shorter time frame, including some goals I hoped to fulfill during my upcoming travels. But even larger than these was my desire to become a more established author with a series of books I was writing. With a sense of excitement about my track record so far, I wondered if the dolphins' tools could be used to manifest these more expansive goals in the brief window available to me.

testing the insights

To test this, I decided to practice using the dolphins' insights as I set out on a series of trips with the goal of fulfilling four of my larger dreams. My goals included having special experiences with the Australian dolphins and whales during the Sixth International Dolphin and Whale Conference at Harvey Bay. I also wanted to swim with the famed spotted dolphins in Bimini and the humpback whales in the Silver Banks off of the Dominican Republic during an upcoming trip. And finally, I wanted to pet the notoriously friendly gray whales in San Ignacio, Mexico, in my second attempt at this experience. Because I had already experienced so many years of cetacean encounters, I understood the potential for sitting in the middle of a vast ocean wondering where all the dolphins and whales had gone, an experience many people have after traveling long distances to see them. Thus, I realized that my dreams were not small and would need to manifest in short time frames, but with my new tools I believed I could fulfill them.

australia

When I got to Australia, I found their boat captains to be so effective in their approach to whale-watching that I was not required to overcome any of the poor conditions I had encountered in Hawaii and on an American cruise in Mexico. Consequently, holding the dream of meeting with the whales happily in my heart was a good deal easier and produced many wonderful experiences. (For information on how Australians attract such successful encounters, see the guidelines on page xiv.)

The only time I was even mildly challenged on this trip occurred during a whale-watching excursion that included among its passengers a king of one of the South African provinces who had spoken in behalf of indigenous people at the conference. He was accompanied by his sister and several English-speaking women, and, perhaps owing to his presence, passengers on the boat were quite subdued and seemed resistant to any playful activities. After an hour without any encounters, a young girl from the South African party who was sitting next to me began to plead with her mother to call to the whales. Her mother shook her head "no" several times, accompanied by a beseeching look that indicated she was not to ask again. But the girl persisted several more times. Then giving up on her mother, she began to tap her hands on the side of the boat.

In spite of the conservative group aboard, I decided to encourage this young girl's playfulness and joined her in her tapping. Almost immediately, two whales produced a tandem spy-hop not far from our boat. And although most of the passengers continued to remain solemn, the girl and I were now cheering while we tapped our drumbeats out on the side of the boat as the whales drew closer. When the girl again pleaded with her mother to call, her mother then surrendered and opened her throat to release the most beautiful trill. The whales got very excited and responded with new, more playful behaviors as they drew even closer to our boat. Most of the group began to quickly relax and enjoy this special encounter until it was cut short by our need to return to the harbor. To my surprise, the whales followed us for a while as the woman continued to trill. This vignette graphically supports the dolphins' view that playing while we wait enhances our attractiveness and helps to pull our dreams to us. I was later able to put this lesson to good use on my trip to Bimini.

bimini

Arrangements were in place for a short flight by seaplane to Bimini Island, where my first husband and I would use a narrow, two-day window to connect with Bimini's famed spotted dolphins who live and play in the waters over the area where the sunken continent of Atlantis is believed to be located.

Yet, as we were waiting to board our seaplane, we received a phone call indicating that things might be turning against us. The weather had been bad at Bimini, and we were forced to cancel one of the days we had scheduled, narrowing our window for meeting with the dolphins to only one afternoon. In addition, the boat owned by the people I had carefully selected to serve as our escorts had been damaged in the weather and was on the blocks for repairs.

I began to dive into my disappointment and fear that things weren't going as required if we were to be successful in swimming with the Bimini dolphins. But I caught myself, interrupted these thoughts, and returned to focusing on my desire to connect with the dolphins instead. Thus, rather than fall into the familiar trap of despair, I pictured myself playing with the famous spotted Bimini dolphins, believed to be the Tibetans among dolphins. I imagined them swimming toward me, alongside me, and inviting me to join them in a playful swim. After a period of immersion in these positive pictures, I not only felt lighter and more joyful, but I had also preserved my attractiveness to the dolphins I yearned to draw to me.

As I sat in this reverie waiting for our seaplane, I noticed right outside my window in the waterway that a dolphin was waving his tail at me. It seemed almost surreal to see this unexpected and humorous sight, much like the distant chirp that had encouraged me to hold on to my faith the day the Hawaii dolphins were on their way to see me. I was so startled by the appearance of this lone dolphin in the narrow waterway that I went to the counter to ask if dolphins typically came into this area. They responded that an occasional dolphin might show up but that it was a fairly rare event.

Following this good omen, we received a call with the news that our contact on Bimini had arranged an alternative boat for us with the only other captain on the island who knew how to connect with the dolphins. However, they warned that, unlike themselves, this captain did not believe in telepathic communication with the dolphins and would simply drive his boat to the area and hope for the best. Rather than fall into the trough of doubt that this captain would not be as good as our original escorts, I held my focus once again on the goal and stayed with it throughout our flight to the island.

When our seaplane touched down at Bimini, the wind was brisk and cold. No boats had gone out that day, and the villagers were uncharacteristically in sweaters and jackets. After touring the island and dining at a local restaurant, we bundled up and retired for the night. The temptation to feel discouraged lurked in the shadows of my mind, but I remembered the dolphins' lesson and maintained my focus instead. Thus, I dropped off to sleep that night, successfully holding the famed spotted dolphins happily in my heart.

When we awakened the following day, the sun shone brightly through the cloudless sky upon a calm blue ocean. Our captain launched his boat in the still, clear waters to begin our journey to the area where others had met with the illustrious Bimini dolphins. However, my husband and I were soon quarreling, and I feared that our discord would interfere with the good fortune I so strong-ly sensed was coming toward us. But rather than get engaged in our problem as I normally would, I separated myself and began to get quiet within. Before long, I was not only holding on to my faith in good things happening to me but was able to send him good wish-es as well.

Focus and faith now filled my heart with contentment, and I felt myself begin to relax. My eyes closed lazily as I lay back against the bow of the boat and surrendered to my knowing that the dol-phins were on their way. No further ripples of fear or doubt dis-turbed my confidence, and I rested peacefully in this faith for the next twenty minutes or so.

I was then startled out of my dreamy state when I heard a voice call out, "There they are!" When I roused myself to look, I saw at least thirty dolphins jumping and playing out ahead. The skipper was surprised by how many dolphins there were and kept exclaim-ing that all three pods had joined together to greet us. He maneu-vered his boat perfectly, providing a respectful and parallel distance between us. As a result. the dolphins soon bounded toward the boat and turned to play in our bow and wake waves.

I could now see some spotted dolphins as well as a few com-mon and bottle-nosed dolphins, including many adults, several adolescents, and a few babies among them. They seemed to be enjoying the waves our boat provided, so I asked the skipper if he would be willing to continue to create these waves as our gift to the dolphins. But he slowed down instead and suggested we get in. I let him know I wanted to give the dolphins a chance to play longer until they seemed more satisfied and finished with this activity. He was concerned that they wouldn't stay with us and that we might miss our swim. But I sensed the dolphins were appreciating the generosity of our gift and would stay and play for as long as we wished following their wave riding. After convinc-ing the captain to continue, we spent the next twenty minutes whooping and hollering as the Bimini dolphins surfed and played in our bow and wake waves.

Then they stopped and milled around the boat, letting us know they were ready for a swim. As we prepared to enter the water, the skipper shared that these dolphins loved people to be as active and innovative as possible. And so we were challenged for the next hour to keep up with these delightfully playful dolphins. When I first got into the water, it seemed as though all thirty dolphins instantly surrounded me, bumping into each other and me in order to get closer. I had never experienced such a cordial encounter. Then one of the dolphins stood upright before me for about a half a minute as we exchanged bows and messages from the heart, each honoring the other. Next, I saw my husband enter the water and dive beneath the surface. The dolphins gathered around him, and he could barely surface without bumping into them.

The dolphins chirped and squeaked and swam toward us and beside us; they raced in circles around us; they brought grass and leaves for us to play with; they invited us to dive with them; they held hands when we did; and they gathered below us all together, sending clicks of sonar up to us. When I asked if they would send a bubble, one instantly released a large one right to me. A second dolphin released another bubble when I thought about bubbles again. Another dolphin caught this bubble in his mouth and popped it. The more we dove, the more the dolphins liked it. One group did the helix spin beneath me; others blew more bubbles; some jumped and somersaulted; and still others snuggled in pairs and threes as they gazed at us. We were blasted until saturated by this welcoming spirit of love and joy.

And so we played and danced with these delightful dolphins until we were out of breath and could dance no more. Only then did they say their good-byes and begin to leave the area. Yet even after we had returned to the boat and begun our trip back to shore, a number of them followed us for a while longer. The skipper kept expressing his amazement at the greeting we had received, the amount of time the dolphins had spent with us, and the unusual number of bubbles the dolphins kept blowing. He exclaimed that on a scale of ten, we had just experienced a nine. He further remarked on how impressed he was that all three pods had joined together to greet us.

When I asked what would have made the experience a ten, he said having more babies in the group, since they get so excited and jump repeatedly for the swimmers. As soon as he said that, a group of three dolphins began to jump repeatedly out ahead of us. At first we thought they were babies, but soon we realized they were adolescents—possibly imitating babies in a humorously dolphin-like manner so as to give us the full ten experience. As we headed back for shore, we agreed that it had been one of our more fulfilling encounters with dolphins, and we were steeped in bliss and feeling wonderfully grateful. I was thankful I had remembered to use the dolphins' manifesting tools and reflected on having created yet another great experience by employing them.

The Bimini encounter had given me the practice I needed for using the dolphins' tools to create whatever dreams I dared to dream. Little did I know how much I would draw from this experience in the next few days to overcome some even more challenging conditions that we would encounter in the Caribbean on the Silver Banks off the Dominican Republic. There I would seek to fulfill my dream of swimming with whales for the first time.

the silver banks

After swimming with dolphins, which are technically small whales, I developed a desire to swim with the larger humpback whales. So I arranged a trip to the world's largest humpback birthing and calving nursery on the Silver Banks with a man who used a respectfully "soft" or quiet entry in these foreign waters where whale encounters are legal.

Getting to the Silver Banks was not easy, nor did I find it an adventure for sissies. We were the oldest people in our party, and I had one near-mishap that verged on serious when I fell into rough water between the tender and the mother boats as they slammed back and forth at each other in choppy waters. But I managed to duck their slams by diving deep under the tender in the same manner I had learned to dive under the waves while surfing as a child in Hawaii. I was then able to get back on board with only a shoulder wrench, and because I so deeply longed to swim with these whales, nothing was going to dissuade me—not even a pulled shoulder. Yet, it was a good thing my focus was so strong, since there were other distractions that vied for my attention throughout the trip as well.

We had boarded the boat in Puerto Plata that would serve as our home for a week on the Silver Banks. The boat ran all night, enabling us to awaken the next morning to a beautiful sunrise. However, tensions started early the first day, as people jockeyed to be placed with the most compatible group, which we had been told would remain fixed for the week, but would alternate between the two small tender boats that would take us closer to the whales. Our group was primarily made up of successful professionals who were individually very engaging but did not work well together as a group.

As a result, our first afternoon produced no encounters, in stark contrast to a swim with five dolphins and two whales reported over dinner by the more easygoing group from the other small boat. This caused our group to feel even more concern about our ability to attract whales, and I could feel the apprehension rising. Consequently, I spent my time before dropping off to sleep that night focusing on seeing whales the following day in spite of these indications to the contrary.

Fortunately, the captain of the alternate tender boat was able to get our group to loosen up a bit and attract some breaches quite close to our boat, which united us in joy. With this, the whales came closer as we cheered louder, and they gave us a dramatic breaching show for the next half hour to our delighted hoots and hollers.

While in the middle of this show, we received a call from the other boat inviting us to join them in an extended underwater interaction they were having with a mother and her calf and escort. We arrived to see the mother floating twenty feet beneath the surface on her back with her pectoral fins outstretched in an open gesture as if to welcome us into her heart and ocean home. It was a moment of great majesty, and I was overcome with tears as I floated above her with my arms shadowing her fins. I floated there for the next half hour, mesmerized, as she remained in this ecstatic pose, her calf mimicking it from beneath her while peeking out at the people from time to time. Her escort stayed quietly nearby, watching us closely as he patiently indulged her kindness to the people. Although I initially felt some fear about swimming with a whale that size, my pounding heart was quickly calmed by her gentle, welcoming energies. The mother whale ended this hour-long encounter by slowly turning to her side, careful not to hit any swimmers or catch them in her slipstream as she fluttered her forty feet of whale tonnage away from us.

Even though our group was more relaxed following this magnificent experience, a growing sense that the other group was better at attracting whales than ours could not be overlooked, and our group began to feel like the "losers" in an undeclared and invisible competition. The leader inadvertently contributed to our growing pessimism by playfully asking who in our group was causing "the problem." Not surprisingly, the lack of group attractiveness that resulted from this tension continued to affect our encounters, and although we enjoyed a number of topside shows, in the next few days I experienced only one underwater encounter, albeit a wonderful experience of gazing into a calf's eyes for about five minutes.

On the final day, I decided to release my goal of creating group synergy and branch out on my own to focus on manifesting more underwater encounters. By releasing the group, I was better able to focus on the tools the dolphins had taught me and started by striving to become more attractive to the whales. I did this by releasing the collective worries and doubts of the group and filling my own heart with love. I then focused only on drawing whales to me rather than entertaining the doubts about whether or not this was possible under the circumstances.

Before long, a series of whales began to approach our boat. When they showed up, I showed up as well by getting into the water more quickly. Our leader had tried all week to persuade our group to get in as soon as the whales approached us, but we had been slow to respond. Now I found myself in the water all alone, face-to-face with a mother and calf who were so close to me my heart began to race. This pair was followed by other mothers with their calves floppily riding their backs and staring into my eyes with their large soulful gazes, as well as one escort swimming ten feet below me, looking enough like a gliding building to make my heart catch in amazement and fear.

After six of these wonderful encounters, we heard a whale singing so loudly his song traveled through the hull of our boat. When I got in the water and made tonal sounds in response, the whale mimicked each sound and waited for the next one, just as the humpbacks in Hawaii had done. This went on for quite a while as the whale drew closer and closer. At one point, he seemed so close I was surprised I couldn't see him. So I put my head up to ask if the two men who had joined me in the water knew where he was. With that I looked to the left and saw his tail thrust very high out of the water waving back and forth as he hung there for several minutes. This was a behavior I had seen on only one other occasion, and it seemed as if the whale had not only answered my question but was teasing us.

When the whale then slipped beneath the surface again, the three of us dove down as well. Next, the whale made a shift from the high tones he had been exchanging with me to a very deep, low tone. The vibration from this tone ran through all three of us with such impact in our chests that we each broke through the water exclaiming, "Did you feel that?!" The whale then waved his tail again and left on that note, but he had made it clear to all of us that if he had sent a stronger blast, he could have exploded our lungs. As a result of personally receiving and experiencing what this sonar felt like, when I later learned of our military sonar in the ocean, I immediately understood its greater threat to life than others seemed to initially grasp.

Although the shoulder injury which had resulted from my fall the preceding day had been growing worse, following our time with the singing whale I was completely pain-free and never noticed the shoulder again. I was also drenched in euphoria as I returned to the boat.

By now the rest of my group had their gear on and were ready to get into the water. I was reminded by their lateness in getting mobilized in time for this amazing experience of the dolphins' lesson about the importance of showing up for your dreams. This remarkable day had shown me how well it works to hold the dream in your heart and show up for it when it arrives. Our next and final encounter was with dolphins and whales playing together, and everyone aboard showed up promptly to participate in this joyful encounter.

On that last night before our departure early the next morning, a number of whales drew near our boat right at sunset, offering repeated, multiple good-bye waves with their pectoral fins and tails. I marveled once again at the conscious nature of cetaceans and smiled at the success of this trip and my growing skills in manifesting my dreams.

san ignacio

On our first evening in San Ignacio, the beautiful Mexican whale nursery was stunning. The lagoon was filled with multiple shades of turquoise, lavender, heliotrope, and blue, offset by white birds flying against the backdrop of pale yellow mountains and a luminous moon. The sun set in oranges and reds over our pristine outhouses, rustic tents, and bags of shower-water warming in the cool evening sun. Nobody complained of our conditions, and only the sounds of oohs and aahs between the clicks of camera shutters could be heard.

The following morning, we set out early in pongas steered by Mexican guides to meet with the famed and friendly San Ignacio gray whales. We found ourselves in a six-person ponga amidst only twelve other pongas allowed on the lagoon at any one time. The passengers in these boats had all traveled from afar for a special whale experience, and our collective hopes and worries were mounting.

Our ponga was filled with a successful and genteel businessman, his beautiful veterinarian wife, and a healthcare worker and her elderly mother, who had sneaked out of town without her doctor's permission in order to kiss a whale before she died. It seemed the whales were everywhere in the lagoon, yet they were eluding the boats while the scent of worry began to fill the air. I noted with disappointment that some of the Mexican boatmen were chasing the whales more than they had during our trip to another part of Baja three years earlier, and I felt disappointed that commercialism had altered their previously more respectful and effective approach.

I quickly released my irritation over this while the others on our boat began to relax and chat among themselves. After learning that the veterinarian also believed in telepathy among animals and used it in her practice, I was reminded to put my awareness in my heart and focus on calling the whales. Before long, I was in the right state for drawing the whales to me, mixed with the faith that they would come. This time, it had taken only a few moments to release my tensions and attain this harmonious yet focused and faithful state, and I noted that the dolphins' tools were becoming second nature to me.

Soon, a mother whale marked by nature with a white, iris-shaped star on her side and a calf with a matching star surfaced near the bow of our boat where I was sitting. Then they popped up together in a dual spy-hop. Next, the calf drew closer and began to spy-hop repeatedly by himself. He then began to flirt with us by rolling over playfully on his side. His mother soon joined him, and they flirted with our boat for the next half hour.

Our particular boatman knew how to approach them skillfully at a parallel angle while keeping a respectful distance. Once we were comfortably close to the whales, he stopped but kept his engine idling, which allowed them to keep auditory tabs on our position and safely approach us. Before long they came within a few inches of our hands outstretched to pet them.

I began to send even stronger waves of love from my heart toward the mother and her calf, while yearning for them to draw near enough for me to actually touch and pet them. The calf got closer and closer, watching me carefully before retreating and then drawing closer again, with occasional nudges from his mother. I held the magnetic force I had created between us, and, eventually, he came alongside the boat. Finally, the calf's head rose slowly up and out of the water right under my hand just as I had visualized, pausing there as I caressed his velvety crown.

Next, he raised his head all the way out of the water until it reached my face, which was now hanging over the bow to greet him. Again I was reminded of St. Francis of Assisi's message that what you yearn for also yearns for you as I petted and hugged this calf, who seemed as interested in my love as I was in his. He repeated this gesture several times and was soon joined by his mother. We played for about an hour in all with Iris, as we later named the mother, and her adorable calf. Our guide noted that she had seen this mother and calf pair earlier in the season but had never seen them approach a boat for petting. Although that week I petted many more whales, saw multiple breaches and bubbles, watched the elderly woman kiss her whale, and even had a whale playfully blow a snout full of water right into my face, this encounter was special, since I knew I had pulled these whales to me by applying the dolphins' lessons.

On my return to the United States, I thought of how wonderful our society and world could be if we used our children's time at school to teach them such things as the dolphins' insights for manifesting their dreams.

a golden heart, a golden life

the sixth insight:

jump only for joy—with freedom and grace

Live only your truth to protect your freedom and joy.

After returning home from my wonderfully fulfilling trips, I jumped quickly back into the busyness of my life. Before long my morning program had become brief, if I fit it in at all, and I spent little or no time focusing on my dreams. Although I was more alert to interrupting negative prophecies about my future and the discouraged feelings that followed, actively focusing on what I did want was no longer a part of my day. Like a monk who has come down from the peace of his mountain to the bustle of the city, I found it harder to stay with my focusing program and, not surprisingly, my dreams were not manifesting as well as they had on my trips.

The first obstacle I noticed to manifesting my next, even larger dreams was my failure to carve out enough time in my schedule for my morning focusing program as well as my failure to protect this time like the golden key to my future that it was. Because I had just experienced how much these practices had helped me to manifest my travel dreams, I could better see how neglecting them was weakening my ability to attract my next dreams to me.

Thus, the first correction I made was to vow never to miss another day of some form of my program and commit to a minimum of one hour a day. Whenever I give even more time to this, my life is enormously empowered, but when I keep it short for extended periods or completely break my vow, I can see the loss of power to my life within a few days. In the process of stopping and starting this program, I have become even clearer about how critical it is to manifesting my dreams.

A second obstacle to manifesting my dreams was the challenge I felt in responding to a publishing offer I had received for this book while I was first learning and practicing the dolphins' tools. Although the publisher was large in both size and stature, and I was pleased with having pulled such a renowned name to me, their communications and offer seemed unduly out of balance. Even though it is standard for unknown authors to accept these arrangements in order to be published, I had reservations about entering into such an unequal partnership for my second book. Yet, it was also hard to let it go, and I fell into confusion.

I couldn't find a clear answer to my dilemma in the manifesting tools I had been given to date and wanted to see if the dolphins had an opinion on what I should do. So I decided to drive out to the bay. I wasn't sure if the dolphins would respond to my inquiry, as this was the first time I was the initiator of a subject between us, but I proceeded nonetheless since the book was about them and their lessons for humanity.

jump only for joy

Upon my arrival I was drawn to the cliff, where I noticed dorsal fins bobbing in the water below me. I parked quickly, then pulled my things together, set up my chair, and asked my question before sitting down. Instantly, an adult dolphin leaped about ten feet into the air. This jump was accompanied by a stronger than usual message: "Jump for joy." Although I was delighted by this surprisingly high jump, the message didn't make sense to me, and I was perturbed that the dolphins were behaving like tricksters when I was in the middle of such an important issue. However, the dolphin repeated his leap into the air, and this time I heard the idea clearly in my mind to "write the book for joy." Then with a shiver, I suddenly understood.

I had often nagged the captive dolphins to jump for joy as they had done when they were free. In captivity, they had of course been conditioned to jump for rewards, but I felt certain that if they could retain their taste for the innate fun of jumping, just for jumping's sake, they would feel happier, even in captivity. Then one day, Keola startled me by leaping out of the hotel's lagoon in response to this mental suggestion and landing sloppily with a free-falling belly flop before me. It looked more shocking than I had anticipated to see a captive dolphin jumping between shows just for the joy of it and also claiming the freedom to do a belly flop similar to those I had seen so often in the wild. We looked at each other for a moment after he surfaced, both of us grinning yet stunned. Neither of us was used to this, and after a few more moments of looking at each other, I threw my head back and began to laugh. Keola held his twinkling eye contact with me as he studied my face and seemed to enjoy both my laughter and understanding of what had just happened.

Now, the wild dolphins were offering me the same suggestion I had offered Keola. But this time in the context of writing my book, urging me to write not with my eye on how fair my reward would be but *simply for the joy of it*. Suddenly, I could see both the humor and wisdom of this idea, and I called out "I got it!" to the dolphins bobbing below as I laughed at their ironic humor and delightful sixth insight.

Although I was grateful for the insight, I didn't want to include this topic in the book, for it initially seemed off the subject of manifesting and also overly personal. Yet, I was repeatedly directed to include it. In my effort to understand why, it dawned on me that the dolphins' answer had been uniquely astute. Only then did I fully absorb the idea that writing the book without regard for my reward would liberate me to act as freely as I had as a child without needing to please others or get paid for my efforts. It had already taken years to put this book together, but I now realized that if I could recapture the feeling of freedom from reward just as I had coaxed the dolphins to do, I would be liberated to write my books freely from my heart for no reason other than the joy I originally felt when I first became a writer.

During my childhood years of innocence, before equivocation and accommodation took hold in my soul, I was better able to act as I deeply believed, without fear of judgment or lack of rewards. This kind of freedom, if claimed by each of us, would allow us to live purely as our higher selves rather than make personal, societal, and world decisions based on a desire to be liked or to protect our income, jobs, status, or power. I realized that this idea was not only useful for me personally but struck deep at the core of how humanity could, as the dolphins do, make decisions based on our true values rather than on those things that money rewards.

Now, focused more fully on the deeper purpose of my authorship and books than on my reward or what it said about my worth as a writer, I accepted the modest fee the publisher offered for my efforts in order to secure an audience for the dolphins' story. The shift in my perception and feeling of freedom and exhilaration it generated within me made me feel as if I too could jump just for the joy of it. And the next weeks were filled with free, fluid writing, simply because I love to write.

Then my contract arrived with additional signals that I might be discounted in other ways and the book put in limbo. When my counterproposals and effort to communicate were met with impatience and surprise at my desire to function as an equal in the relationship, the arrangement began to feel unworkable for me. Yet, it was still hard to give up such a large publisher interested in the dolphins' story. Besides, I understood that the publisher was not doing anything unusual or considered in the industry to be "wrong." They were merely acting in accordance with what had become the standard publishing approach to non-celebrity authors in our society. But I wasn't used to such unequal social status in my relationships or being treated with such disdain. And so I continued to struggle with my decision.

The following day, I went back to the dolphins to see what they had to say. When I arrived, they were again waiting at the cliff. But this time their energy was solemn and there were no jumps of joy. Another strongly delivered message indicated that jumping for joy is natural and easy whenever you are free. But although it can still be done, it's considerably harder anytime you have lost your freedom. Thus, it's always better whenever possible to *arrange for your equality and freedom in advance*. This was the most complex thought the dolphins had ever transmitted to me, and it constituted the second aspect of their sixth and final insight.

As I pondered this idea, I was reminded of the intensely sad dolphin who had impressed the pain of his captivity on us, demonstrating that he had not won the battle to feel joyful without the equal status and freedom he yearned for. I thought too of how Iwa had unfailingly given her gift of love and healing for years before succumbing to depression when her needs were blatantly discounted and she was separated from her family to be placed in a small and crowded pen. I thought of Maka, who cheered me up during my separation and has cheered and healed so many others, spending two years in painful seclusion as punishment for becoming slightly less cooperative under the tutelage of an unskilled trainer. I further thought of how, in my years of exposure to captive dolphins, I had never seen any of them except Keola jump between shows simply for the joy of it as the wild dolphins so often do in the freedom of the open ocean. And I thought of the thousands of dolphins and whales who had not been able to prevail in captivity without their equality and freedom but had died, committed suicide, or become depressed and ill as a result of their pain.

My thoughts turned to the equally scant number of humans who have been able to survive years of captivity with their spirits intact and how we deeply honor and respect those who have, such as the famed Viktor Frankl, who was imprisoned in Auschwitz as well as three other Nazi death camps. I thought too of the millions in our country and throughout the world who have been discounted and marginalized by others and have not prevailed in the face of it but take antidepressants instead in an often futile attempt to bolster their spirits.

I realized how pervasive the human struggle over dominance, power, status, and money is in our world and the unequal treatment of others this struggle promotes. Even though this attitude can be subtle, it is the most significant error humanity makes and lies at the core of the problems we create for ourselves and others. In fact, it is our inability to view others as if they are as important as ourselves that allows humans not only to discount each other but to ignore the value of the earth and oceans as well as other species sharing them with us.

I could now see why the dolphins had introduced this important sixth insight, since it's a great challenge to feel truly happy, even with the skills of manifesting, if we are not free or treated with equality. I could also see that the dolphins were right: It is better to arrange for this freedom in advance whenever possible. Yet I wondered how many of us would actually hold out for equal status in our business and personal relationships when faced with this human tendency to seek dominance over others.

As fate would have it, I went to a talk by Marianne Williamson that evening on this very subject. To a standing ovation, she encouraged disdained and marginalized people to stop putting up with the unfair terms they are offered in life. As she reviewed the list of those in this category, it included women in general; abused, molested, and neglected children; people from various racial groups, religious beliefs, and sexual orientations; the poor or struggling; and those in demeaning jobs with unfair conditions. It further included people in unequal personal and professional relationships and inequitable business partnerships. And it included the millions afraid to stand up to such violations of the human spirit as the holocaust, slavery, ethnic cleansing, and other crimes of hate as well as the deceit and betrayal of business, science, medicine, law, and government. It also included our treatment of other species and the very planet we claim as our home. The list is endless, and most people fit into at least one of these marginalized categories.

She punctuated her talk by declaring that we don't lack a nation of people with good values and a sense of fairness; we lack a nation of people with the courage to stand up for what they know to be right. In order to gain the courage needed to stand up for equal and free relationships and partnerships, we must first comprehend that we cannot usher in the new world of our dreams without letting go of the lower-self attitudes and outdated rules of a world we must leave behind.

I thought of my unequal publishing contract and realized that what the dolphins had said was not only true but profound: It is better to arrange for your equality and freedom in advance whenever possible. But I also realized why we don't do it. I knew it would be a challenge for me to walk away from such a large publisher just as it is a challenge for others to leave the conditions that bind them to subservient roles. Yet, I also realized that as fearsome as we have come to view claiming full equality in our relationships with others, it is even more horrifying to sign up for our own captivity.

To succeed in surmounting the fears that prevent us from protecting our equality from the outset, we need to realize that standing up for ourselves is not as frightening as we have made it out to be. In fact, it is nothing more than speaking up for what we truly believe rather than allowing the fear of being disdained or disliked or losing our slot in an unequal partnership to silence us.

We must also understand that a hierarchy of status is currently an accepted part of our culture and that we each play our part to keep it in place. As a result, one side isn't more to blame than the other, since we work together to create it. In fact, as I examined this problem in our society, I realized that there are times when I am the one on the dominant side of this unequal arrangement, and I realized how hard it would be for me to give up that role as well. Yet as soon as any one of us drops out of the pattern, it begins to unravel and release. Because those in the dominant position are less likely to initiate the change, those of us on the short end of the arrangement must find the courage to begin. Thus, anytime we feel unequal in our partnerships, we must first wake up and then stand up for ourselves and for our freedom. This is what I had done as a young woman in the early '60s at the beginning of the women's movement, and this is what I needed to do now.

I decided to face my fears and arrange for my own equality and freedom as an author and person in all of my relationships and to do so without indignation or anger, as the dolphins had taught me, but to simply do it. And so I set out the following day to decline the unsatisfactory contract and to either find a more equal partnership or publish the book myself. Upon doing this, I felt free to write my book simply for the joy of it in the context of freedom. Although it took courage to take this step, it also felt right, and the moment I claimed this freedom for my spirit, I felt exuberant. Ideas for the book again flooded through me, and I felt freer, lighter, and happier than I ever had. Even more important, from this new perspective of personal freedom and power I could more clearly see how many people were still in bondage to their fear of claiming this level of equality and freedom in our human society, and I realized the importance of this sixth and final insight.

I could also better understand how free the wild dolphins are in their non-economic and watery world and why they dance with such joy in the seamless ocean. I could further see how they work together in their fluid and open society to fulfill both individual and group needs rather than manipulating each other or jockeying for position as humans do.

selecting my next dream

After releasing the large publisher, I was ready to celebrate my new experience of personal courage and freedom, and I responded to a strong call to play with the dolphins. On my way there, I asked for a sign about whether or not a more equitable publishing partnership would show up, either as a partner in a self-publishing venture or as another publisher. I noticed as I drove that I had no further preferences or concerns about this now that I knew how to claim equality and freedom without fear in my land-based world.

When I arrived, I saw dolphins playing on the surface well beyond the bay and cliff, so I drove in that direction. Then I lost sight of them but found a place to park along the side of the road. After getting tucked into this spot I glanced at the ocean just as two young dolphins rose in perfect synchronization out of the water right on the shoreline where I was parked and then arched their backs to curve their bodies into a rare and beautiful dual back-flip, the first I had seen in tandem. It felt as though they offered a symbolic message that I would draw a harmonious publishing arrangement to me, no matter what form it took. I noticed as I watched this priceless display that all the feelings of smallness and fear I had experienced as an unknown author in the daunting publishing industry were gone, and I felt peacefully aligned with the harmony the dolphins reflected.

gratitude

As I sat in my car absorbing this sign, I saw the dolphins heading toward the bay, so I drove in that direction to go for a swim. When I got into the water, a young dolphin established immediate and constant voice contact with me. I sent out my "yeeha" signature sound, which I thought I heard him mimic. Because none of the dolphins had ever copied this sound over the past ten years of my doing it, I questioned if I had heard him correctly. Then he did it several more times, now more slowly and deliberately echoing the sound of my joy.

Next, I had a special encounter with my closest dolphin friends, who had served as my teachers for the past ten years. To begin, six dolphins gathered around and did the helix spin under me. Following this, a mother with her tiny baby, only a day or two old, swam alongside me for a while. At first, the baby peeked at me from behind his mother and then darted under her to get between us for a few moments before retreating beneath her and trying it again. This was something I had not previously experienced, and I was flooded with gratefulness.

In that moment I realized that gratitude is not something we experience as an afterthought but is a feeling integral to each blessed moment. I also realized that this feeling had been building in me and was a result of a new and positive template which had been set in motion in my life and was now serving as a magnet for more goodness.

I finished the bulk of the book within a week and went to visit the hotel dolphins, whom I had neglected during the writing process. Kaiko'o stood upright before me the moment I arrived, shuddered and smiled, and then dove to the bottom to get a rock, which he held proudly in his mouth while continuing to stand upright before me for a long, twinkle-eyed gaze as visitors snapped pictures of him.

Maka also gave me his attention that day, strutting by with a leaf on his tail, as did Iwa's son, Hoku, who had recently moved to the lagoon with Kaiko'o, and I was enchanted by long periods of gazing into each of their hearts. All three dolphins swirled vortexes through the water with their fins and tails and blew a variety of bubbles. Just as I was preparing to leave, Maka jumped three-quarters of the way out of the lagoon and then came over to bask in my squeals of amazement. A few moments later, Hoku executed the same three-quarter jump. I was astonished that each of these dolphins, whom I had never seen do a free jump, did one that particular day. As I thought about their jumps, I wondered if they were celebrating my own choice for freedom yet were keeping their jumps only three-quarters high because they did not have their own. As always, the dolphins made me wonder how they seemed to understand so much.

When I returned home, I learned that the editor for the large publisher who liked my book was moving to another house. Because this could have put my book in serious jeopardy had I stayed with them, I felt particularly blessed by my decision and the courage and freedom I had learned in the process of making it.

another dream arrives

After another month passed, I was nearing the end of editing my book and pulling it together to go to press. Three new publishers had shown interest in it, but none had followed up, and I was within a few weeks of initiating self-publishing. I felt very peaceful and strong during this period, and even though I had not found a publisher, I continued to follow the steps I had learned from the dolphins. As a result, I was filled with feelings of optimism, freedom, and joy, as well as a steady belief that the best outcome for me and the book would be drawn to my life, whether it was working with a publisher or conducting my own self-publishing venture. Then a large publisher contacted me, followed by a call from another. Within a week, I signed a contract that offered me a publishing partnership.

A week later, I was incorporating some of their editing suggestions and took my book bag filled with the entire manuscript to the beach to work on in the sun. As I walked toward the dolphin pool, I was surprised by an enthusiastic greeting from one of the new dolphins, Kaiko'o. He rushed all the way to the edge of the pool and stood upright before me, looking directly at me with a delighted look on his face. Next, he leaped from the small pool while keeping his eye on me as he jumped, and then he lifted his tail under himself at the end of his leap with an exaggerated motion, as if to emphasize that he was jumping all the way out of the water. I hooted loudly, and he chirped back as people gathered around the pool to see what was happening. Kaiko'o dashed over to the edge again and stood upright before me, looking very pleased with himself as his eyes twinkled happily into mine.

Then, he pulled himself fully from the water again, following the course of his first jump, but this time flipping water at me with his tail before lifting it to clear the water for another full jump. I laughed heartily as our eyes met again in recognition of what this meant. And again he rushed over and stood upright before me, his face alight with pleasure and his chest flushed with pink.

To my amazement, Kaiko'o jumped again, this time coming down with a big splash aimed in my direction that soaked the rocks between us and caused his trainer to later mention the wet area and ask Kaiko'o what was going on. He rushed over to me again and stood upright as I squealed openly with delight and asked if he could feel the joy. Kaiko'o executed two more full jumps, the last one reaching several feet into the air before splashing more water on the rocks. He seemed to be truly enjoying himself as I looked on with amazement and cheered with utter joy.

A sweet man with a heavy foreign accent approached me to ask, "What do you do to make the dolphin sing?" I smiled and clasped the book bag in my hand as I replied, "He's remembering to jump for joy."

jump for joy,
then jump again,
and then again.

PART 4

the future

CHAPTER 16

no more tears:

displacing our biggest problem with love

The tears are there for us to hear so that we can respond.

At the time the first edition of this book was going to press, there was a serious planetary problem brewing beneath the sea, well hidden from most of our view. Although I would normally have cared very deeply about such a problem, I would not have become involved. Yet, because of the singing whale who sent me a close to lung-bursting blast of sonar in the Silver Banks as described earlier, I immediately understood the profundity of the problem and felt I had to explore it further. As a result, I found myself at the center of the issue and reluctantly in a position similar to the one in which Erin Brockovich found herself when she uncovered the toxic waste-dumping scam. Yet, the sonar problem was even more serious than a localized issue of toxic waste dumping and had far broader implications. Although I naively assumed that my involvement would be short-lived and quickly successful, it expanded into several years, which culminated in an amazing story that provided me with my final confirmation of the high level of dolphin and whale consciousness and wisdom. Although others may not agree with the details of the following story as told from my perspective, here is my view of what actually happened.

my first tears

My insight into the degree of human unkindness toward the dolphins and whales began in a dark room on the island of Maui, as I watched a heartbreaking story unfold on the movie screen before me. I was shocked by the sight of five powerful orcas remaining absolutely still in a lagoon off Japan while a handful of men, looking particularly small next to these gentle giants, were puffed up with pride as they tied their ropes around the obliging whales, who could easily have killed the men had they chosen to. While the men proceeded, the orcas' children and other family members watched from an area nearby, steadily screaming the most forlorn cries I have ever heard.

I viewed this film with horror in a darkened room along with a few hundred other shocked men and women attending the 1998 Whales Alive Conference. As I watched, I felt confused not only by the whales' unwillingness to subdue their captors but also by their degree of gentleness with them. Then it slowly dawned on me that I was watching yet another example of kenosis . . . the kind of love expressed in the emptying of all resistance and malice in order to fill the emptiness solely with God's love. It is a model taught by Jesus and practiced by other gentle giants such as Mahatma Gandhi, Martin Luther King, and Nelson Mandela to achieve results that would otherwise seem impossible to attain. It is also practiced regularly by the dolphins and whales as described in this book and was being so powerfully expressed by the five captured orcas that the love of God poured through the whales to fill the room.

Before long, I could hear the sobs of the others blend with mine as we joined the orphaned calves in their grief while being blasted with the love of God flowing through their captured parents. I felt deep shame over being part of the species that was doing this to the whales, and wondered helplessly what I could do to help. Typically and tragically, three of the five orcas captured that day died within a few weeks.

Later in the conference, another speaker moved our hearts with his story of once being in a Greenpeace pontoon situated between a whaling boat and the whale they were pursuing. In response to this obstruction, the boat captain moved so aggressively toward the pontoon that he seriously threatened the lives of the activists defending the whale before continuing past them to fire a harpoon. Now bleeding from the spear's wound driven deep into his skull, the whale made his way over to the pontoon, and just as the brave activists wondered what he would do next, he gently nuzzled his body alongside their boat. He then engaged our speaker in a powerfully loving gaze and with his eyes thanked him for his kindness and caring. He then held this gaze between them until his life force had finished draining from his own kind being, and he slipped beneath the water to his death.

Profoundly moved by this whale's act of self-emptying love as he bobbed before him, completely devoid of all malice and filled only with gratitude for the activist's compassion, the activist dedicated the rest of his life to helping the dolphins and whales.

Over time, I also learned, both at the Whales Alive Conference and on the Internet, of the new brands of sonar in our world's oceans, which were believed at that time by many activists to be highly disruptive to the lives and wellbeing of dolphins and whales. These disturbances were initially assumed to result from the intensity of the sound of the new, more forceful low-frequency sonar blasts—similar to the low, vibrational sound the singing whale had sent to me. Their primary concern was that if the new sound levels were loud enough, they might cause changes in dolphin and whale migration and mating patterns, as well as possible hearing loss, which could lead to collisions with boats, starvation, and slow but eventual extinction.

However, as a result of my experience with the singing whale's blasting me with his own sonar, I could not view the military sonar merely as a sound intensity nuisance as the others were doing but suspected the sonar could cause vibrational resonance strong enough to explode tissue. If so, it posed a far more serious and imminent threat that could result in massive cetacean strandings and deaths as well as a serious threat to all marine life. The thought initially seemed so outlandish that even I had trouble imagining it. But I couldn't turn my back on the enormity of this possibility, so, like the Greenpeace activists and others at the conference, I committed to helping to stop the sonar. Little did I know when I did this, however, that I would find myself at odds not only with those who wanted to use this new technology but also with the activists who opposed it.

Following is the story of how my long-disputed hypothesis was eventually proven correct, and how this was verified with the dramatic, almost unbelievable help of the dolphins and whales. Yet, in spite of this proof and the subsequent laws passed to prevent the military sonar's use, the sonar remains in the water—as a result of several loopholes—doggedly continuing to threaten all marine life and possibly the ocean itself. If this continues, it could serve as the blueprint for our own self-destruction, yet we persist in remaining asleep. My hope is that my sharing more of this story, the mystery that surrounds it, and the miraculous role the dolphins and whales played in surfacing the truth of it will inspire others to finally awaken and respond to resolving it.

the sonar story through my eyes

Following my singing whale experience in 1997 and the awareness of the use of worldwide sonar in our oceans that I gained at the Whales Alive Conference, I began to investigate what was going on.

One of the first things I learned was that the Marine Mammal Commission had written into an early report on sonar that the new brands of this technology are capable of causing tissue explosion in marine mammals and would extensively threaten all marine life if it was used throughout the world's oceans as planned.

Although their prediction matched my hypothesis, their condemning information and early warning against using the sonar was buried in an obscure report and seemed to be purposely ignored in the assessment process of sonar safety. As a result, very few people seemed to know about this report or the probability of sonar-induced tissue explosion that the report proposed.

I also learned from another source that if the ears of stranded whales were carefully tested, the tests would reveal whether or not their vulnerable ear cavities had exploded as a result of acoustic assault, which would confirm—or disprove—any link between the strandings and sonar exposure.

I initially assumed the National Marine Fisheries Services (NMFS), a government agency formed to protect our oceans, would make it a priority to check the ears of whales exposed to sonar in order to gain this important information, but I soon learned that they refused to do so, even when the whale carcasses were fresh or when activist groups offered to pay for the ear removals and tests. Instead the NMFS preferred to conduct less comprehensive tests or drag the dead whales out to sea to sink without doing any tests whatsoever. They would then report to the media that the deaths were a "mystery" under investigation and blame it on things "out of our control" such as red algae bloom, even when no blooms were in the area.

I then learned there was a loophole in the Marine Mammal Act of 1972 that said if anyone caused harm to the ocean or marine life but was not aware of the harm they were inflicting, they would not be culpable. This loophole, coupled with NMFS's puzzling lack of interest in the problems of sonar-exposed whales, pointed to the possibility that they wanted protection from knowing the extent of the sonar's harm because the NMFS was serving more as a partner in the promotion of this powerful technology than an overseer, determining its safety.

Over the next few years, the more I learned, the more I became aware that this force was already operating in our oceans without proper permits or restraints. I also learned that the Natural Resources Defense Counsel (NRDC)—which had attracted a number of eminent members opposed to the sonar, such as the late John

Kennedy, Jr,. his cousin Robert Kennedy, Pierce Bronson, James Taylor, and Jean-Michel Cousteau—had sued the navy for doing this illegally. Yet even their concerns about it at that time seemed focused on the usual anguish regarding the lesser problem of the noise factor.

deciding what to do

Amidst rumors that the sonar was outmoded and not really needed except possibly as a powerful underwater weapon, I became unsure of what to do with my knowledge of its dangers. And so I tried objectively to weigh the perceived need for sonar against its danger to our futures.

I began by charting the pattern of strandings of dolphins and whales that had been in the vicinity of sonar exercises just prior to their deaths. To my dismay, I learned that even though deployment of this operation was barely underway, it was creating a wide swath of death and destruction in its path.

I also learned that in addition to the dead cetaceans we knew about, there were many others lying buried in a growing graveyard on the ocean's floor. In addition, I learned of a rise in worldwide reports of "mysterious" deaths of dolphins and whales and other marine life, including fish.

This threat to marine life brought me to the further conclusion that if the problematic sonar was used in 70 to 80 percent of the world's oceans in accordance with the declared goal of those promoting it, such wide use of this lethal force would indeed create the potential for it to kill all marine life as well as the ocean itself.

It was then that I first realized with alarm that the sonar was not just another environmental nuisance but challenged humanity with its greatest crisis and possible self-destruction. My assumptions were no longer outlandish. The sonar was proving to be a serious threat to all of us. And I wondered what choice I really had but to awaken others to this possibility.

Yet, I also had a conflict. I had been close to many high-ranking naval officers, including a number of well-known admirals and their families, while growing up on a plantation in Hawaii that had a close connection with the naval base adjoining it. I knew better than most that these were good people, and I was confused as to why they were pursuing such a damaging technology. But then it occurred to me that in an effort to support their cause, their own science had probably failed to root out the real dangers of the sonar. I also believed that if they understood the full impact of the resonance factor, they would more aggressively pursue alternatives to this lethal technology.

Although I felt even more lonely in my perception of the additional power created by the resonance, I also felt I had a moral responsibility to continue to expose it in the event that I was right. And so I mustered up my courage to print my findings on the Internet in an article called "Beware the Beached Canaries," which was widely circulated and reached many thousands of people.

enlisting help

I then contacted the now deceased Congresswoman Patsy Mink to let her know what I had uncovered. My father had helped Patsy Mink get into office in the early days of her political career in Hawaii, and I decided to now call on that marker to get through. Patsy Mink responded as I had hoped and brought the issue to the awareness of her fellow political leaders in Congress, which helped to prime them to pay more attention to subsequent information on the topic.

understandable disagreement with the activists

Next, I tried again to get through to the activist group who was now vigorously ignoring me because of their unhappiness with my broadly disseminated "Beached Canaries" article claiming that sonar could kill whales and possibly the ocean itself.

Because I was the first among them to believe that sonar had a potential for greater harm than they originally perceived, my position put us at odds. Yet, it was understandable that, without their having experienced the strength of the sonar vibration as I had with the singing whale, this concept would seem absurd to them. It was also understandable that, if we continued to be associated, my public declaration of such an "outlandish" idea would affect their credibility with the navy and NMFS scientists. And these were the people they hoped to persuade to stop their use of sonar with their research and with arguments against introducing such loud and disturbing sounds in the ocean, which they believed at that time to be the primary problem. Because of these factors, it's not surprising that my efforts to get reconnected with them failed.

In fact, to distance themselves even further from my openly declared opinion, the activists publicly declared that sonar could not possibly kill whales and that the idea it might kill the ocean was patently absurd. In addition, most of the activists disassociated themselves from my "nonsense" by excluding me from their group and email conversations, which I had previously been privy to.

the video

In spite of this snubbing, two of the activists who agreed with my viewpoint made important contributions to the ultimate disclosure of this serious problem, one with a video revealing more—though not the full extent—of the problem and the other using her D.C. connections to get this video distributed to Congressional leaders. This, coupled with Patsy Mink's contribution, provided a valuable foundation of awareness in the minds of political leaders, which created enough soil for later events to get seeded and take hold.

the importance of checking the ears

Rather than back off, I remained relentless. And so anytime some-one in the group inadvertently included me in an email communi-cation, I used the opportunity to remind them to do whatever they could to get the whales' ears checked—since this would be their most efficient way to establish the connection between cetacean sonar exposure and the explosion of their body cavities and ulti-mate death.

Not surprisingly, I was increasingly shunned by almost every-one in the activist group and received no further information from them until one day early in February of 2000, when I was inadver-tently included in a vital email. This communication announced a shocking increase in strandings throughout the world in places where the sonar activities were known to be taking place, and the dolphins and whales were managing to get to shore to strand and be counted.

"no more tears/check the ears"

I knew this would probably be my last chance to speak to the entire inner circle of activists and decided that the most important thing I could impress on them was the need to get these particular whales' ears checked. So I offered a simple ditty to these serious sci-entists, which simply and directly reminded—"If you want no more tears, then check their ears." I added, "Sing to any tune . . . but keep singing."

I knew my ditty would appear as the final evidence to the group that I was indeed the lightweight "ninny" they had assumed me to be. But I also knew that the suggestion to check the whales' ears embedded in this irritating song—much like a disagreeable adver-tisement—would catch in their awareness and thus be highlighted and remembered primarily for its ability to annoy.

Planting this idea in the minds of the only group of environ-mental scientists in a position to help get the ear tests accomplished came too late for the February 2000 strandings. However, the idea was well-seeded in their minds and lurked on each of their radar screens in better readiness for the dramatic events that followed a month later in March of 2000.

the turning point

By early March of 2000, the NMFS had managed to get by the activists and red tape to approve the permits for as many allowable whale deaths as were needed for the navy to use the sonar, and all was in place for full deployment of this powerful, yet untested technology to be used broadly in our world's oceans. It appeared that those who were concerned about the sonar had lost their battle, and this greatest of all threats to our planet was poised for unveiling.

I felt uniquely alone in my awareness of the true power of the sonar, and I spent a good deal of time in prayer over it. I also used the manifesting program the dolphins had shared with me to pull to this earth visions of a sonar-free ocean filled with vitally joyful dolphins and whales and thriving marine life. Then one day, I felt a sudden sense of relief about the sonar and cried hard as I surrendered my trust to God to handle it. I slipped into a state of peace and felt "empty" of the problem as well as my worries and sadness about it.

I noticed as I did this that it felt as if the dolphins and whales had joined me in my heart and prayers, and a powerful "sense of things" flooded my awareness—seeming to promise that the sonar issue would be miraculously resolved. It was an odd feeling that I didn't fully understand or share with anyone, but I was able at last to release my worries about the sonar, and when it was over, I felt unusually calm.

Ironically, on March 15 of 2000, about two weeks following this prayerful experience, and just before full deployment of the sonar was about to be launched, it seems the military exercises began prematurely and sixteen sonar-exposed whales and several dolphins found their way to the Abacos shore in the Caribbean.

An even greater irony was that these cetaceans were not only out of the jurisdiction of the NMFS, who had been blocking their ear tests, but landed on the beachfront property of possibly the only maverick marine scientist who was uniquely able to prepare their ears for testing. It seemed clear to me that the dolphins and whales had taken exquisite advantage of this narrow window of opportunity to do their part, and I marveled at the level of consciousness that seemed to be involved in this selection of their landing points.

However, the maverick scientist was also a past navy man, and although he loved the whales with all his heart, he had hoped to avoid engaging in any politics with his beloved navy over the controversial sonar issue. In addition, he was one of the activists who had found me particularly annoying. Yet, as much as he must have hated to admit it, my nattering about getting the ears tested had made him and others aware that getting fresh ear samples had been the most critical missing link in solving the mystery of why the whales were dying. They had all been conforming to the legally required U.S. protocol by calling on the NMFS to handle stranded whales and assumed the appropriate tests were being performed.

However, the NMFS was simply not responding as expected, and thus, absolutely no ear tests had been obtained, even after I had brought to public attention the problem this missing link was causing—which in turn created even more pressure on the NMFS to perform the tests. Although others hated to admit it, I had irritatingly succeeded in bringing this overt NMFS negligence to everyone's attention along with my repeated urging for someone to get the job done!

Now, watching one of the whales before him bleed from the eyes as the whale slowly died on his beachfront property, the scientist's heart was moved in new directions that pulled him off the fence. He was also on foreign soil and outside the jurisdiction of the NMFS, and so decided to remove the whales' heads in preparation for testing their ears. With this decision, he became the person to set in motion the exposure of solid evidence that showed the connection between cetacean sonar exposure and the kinds of mysterious dolphin and whale strandings that had been taking place around the world with increased frequency.

Because he was the one who had prepared these whales' ears for testing, he was also in a position to both watch and videotape the ear-testing experts during the first phase of the tests. He had clearly witnessed with his own eyes (and video camera) the bloody impact of explosive concussions to the ears and brains of these sonar-exposed whales. Thus, when the experts—who were recipients of complex and fettered funding connected to parties favoring the sonar—later seemed to delay and then hedge about their conclusions, he decided to share his observations and tape in a series of national press conferences.

Although this resulted in great personal loss to him, as he was subsequently shunned by his colleagues and denied research applications, the word that the deaths had been caused by the sonar was now out of the bag, both in Congress and with the press, and the clarity of this proof could never be recalled or hidden again. It was a bell that could not be unrung.

This information ultimately led to San Francisco-based U.S. Magistrate Judge Elizabeth De La Porte's issuing a temporary injunction against the use of the sonar, followed by a permanent injunction. After this, US District Judge Samuel Conti issued a permanent injunction against testing the sonar with the Gray whales, based on the NMFS's being proven by plaintiffs to have acted "arbitrarily, capriciously, and in a manner contrary to law" in assigning permits for these tests.

Following these injunctions, Congress passed a bill to suspend use of the sonar. Yet, even with these restraints, those imposing them still did not seem to grasp the full measure of the problem with sonar in our oceans. As a result, this suspension was later overridden by Congressional approval of an exemption—tacked onto a defense bill—for exempting the U.S. military from obeying the Marine Mammal Protection Act and Endangered Species Act provisions as needed for security.

Now, thanks to our wartime status, the sonar has gone back into the water with greater force and less restraint than was previously exercised. As a result, strandings are once again occurring continuously around the world. Yet, this is only the tip of the iceberg, since the ones who are stranding are the ones who have made it to our shores and can be seen and counted, while many more are sinking directly to the ocean's floor without our awareness or opportunity to count them.

My hope is that this story will not only make the citizens of our world aware of what we are doing, but also move their hearts to care and to act. In addition, the story is designed to show that our actions will be most powerful if we employ the power of kenosis, or the kind of love expressed in the emptying of our positions of resistance or malice in order to fill the vacuum this leaves in our hearts solely with God's love—as practiced so abundantly by dolphins and whales. The following images taken from the way the dolphins and whales behave in the world show us how this might work.

crystals and kenosis

Even when we treat the dolphins and whales without kindness, they consistently send their love to us. The power of this can be graphically seen in the water crystals made beautiful by the energy of their kindness and love, as demonstrated in the photos of Dr. Masaru Emoto. This explains why the dolphins would instantly leave the bay whenever the humans swimming in it were filled with unkind thoughts and why they taught me not to send my anger into the bay, even though I had acted on behalf of their protection.

The dolphins and whales have shown us by these and other actions how to steadily practice the art of kenosis, and a vision of the beautiful crystals they were making wherever they were no matter what the conditions, helped to make sense of this high-level choice.

the dolphins' and whales' response to our sonar

At a time when the sonar was going into the ocean on a more regular basis and the Hawaii dolphins and whales were being particularly challenged by these assaults, the orcas in the San Juans were showing up in time for concerts given for their benefit and were actively appreciating and interacting with the human musicians playing for them.

Further down the coast, a super-pod of whales numbering in the thousands showed up off of Dana Point in California. They actively played with people in their leisure boats and in the water for several hours and then stayed with them until sunset, at which time the pod lay still on the surface as the sun set dramatically on a sea filled with their dorsal fins.

In addition, the dolphin rescue of the famed Cuban boy, Elian Gonzales, ironically took place during the time when the sonar was going back into the water.

The dolphins and whales remain primarily kind and gentle with us, forever willing to play and help and teach us no matter what we do to them. Like others who have reached similarly high states of development, they seem to be waiting patiently for our hearts to open and our own consciousness and consciences to awaken. They also seem to know that their presence in our lives will accelerate this process, and so they continue to come to our boats and shores, to seek us out and help us to heal and evolve toward our highest potential—for their survival depends on our hearts being moved enough to behave at a higher level. Yet, they are also clear they will remain who they are, whether or not we succeed.

the film—"no more tears"

Although humans are used to resisting and fighting the things they don't like and want to have improved—such as drugs, fat, poverty, hunger, and now terrorism—I felt that the most important thing I could offer my own species was a new approach to our problems, and kenosis seemed the best option. Although this could be viewed as a strange idea, if we face the truth of things, we would have to admit that our wars have, without fail, made each of our problems worse. So what could we possibly lose by actually trying the power of love, which we have been taught is the way to miracles and moving mountains?

To demonstrate how to accomplish this I wrote a film based on the sonar story as told here, but rather than merely expose it, even with the inclusion of the whales' phenomenal role in that exposé, I decided to visually show how love—rather than resistance, anger, and battles—has the power to rather easily and rapidly displace and resolve this and other serious human problems. The key is to harness and use it, and the film shows us how. My husband wrote a song titled "No More Tears" for the film, and so I decided to give the film the same name.

the bishop

Soon after I completed the film, I learned that the Bishop of Melbourne in Australia is close to a highly visible and successful actor and film producer who has a particular interest in the dolphins and whales—and I wondered if there might be a chance of getting my film to the Bishop to pass on to this actor/producer.

Several months later, we were blessed by a gracious offer of a luxurious free ride to Australia, and the Bishop agreed to meet with us while we were there. The entire trip was filled with gifts from God and nature as well as many wonderful people, all acting as their best and highest selves.

We had photographed many sights, enjoyed many special conversations, given a seminar, and had completed some private consulting. Then, on the eve before we were scheduled to see the Bishop, we were relaxing at a delightful restaurant with our friends. We were already in heaven, grinning from ear to ear and talking and laughing over a fine meal when an acquaintance of our friends came over to say hi. She happened to be the female senior long board surfing champion of Western Australia and shrieked when she realized that I was the author of the first edition of this book describing the conscious nature of dolphins.

She briefly abandoned her own dinner party to sit down to tell us what had happened to her just the day before. She shared that after all her years in the water, she had experienced her first encounter with two wild dolphins who stayed to play and surf with her for over an hour. They even helped her to catch up to a wave she had already missed and get into it in time for the full ride, an experience that was clearly amazing for her. Yet she had no doubt, thanks to her years of surfing experience, that it had in fact happened. She was also amazed that when the dolphins first arrived, it wasn't until she invited them to surf with her that they leaped into the air simultaneously to catch the next approaching wave.

She couldn't believe running into me the day following this experience as she loved the book and kept marveling over the coincidence of meeting its author after playing with the dolphins. As she talked, I realized that the encounter with her was also an omen for me, one that portended that our meeting with the Bishop the next day would go well.

And so it did. Our friends drove us into Melbourne, where we all enjoyed our cups of tea and coffee before heading down a particularly pretty lane lined with old buildings to see the Bishop. He was waiting outside for us and grinned from the end of the lane as he waved his welcome to us.

When my husband and I were married, one of the two people attending was a dear friend, an astute judge, who told us of the Celts' belief that events such as births, weddings, and funerals are "thin" moments that enable us to more easily feel the presence of God. As our friend conveyed this information, the moment instantly and movingly became thin for all four of us, and we were married in the thinness. Similarly, from the time we first saw the Bishop of Melbourne standing in the lane until we said our goodbyes, we experienced another wonderfully thin moment in time.

The Bishop began our meeting by asking my husband to sing the song that he had composed for the film. Although he does not usually like to sing under such circumstances, he happily sang "No More Tears" for the Bishop in his beautiful baritone voice.

Next, the Bishop asked about the film's story and found it interesting. Then he asked what the larger purpose for producing the film might be, and I told him about the examples of kenosis and how the film demonstrated a way to tap this incredible power for use in solving our largest human problems. He looked into my eyes for an extended, dolphin-like gaze that moved all of us to tears. He then picked up the script and promised to share it with his film friend.

Although it was clear that the meeting was over, none of us moved. Finally, I admitted that it was hard to leave his presence, and he chuckled with understanding, while making us feel welcome to stay. As with the dolphins and whales, we were in the presence of a high being. The thing that struck me is that this level of development, whether in dolphins or Bishops, is available to all of us if we will just begin—and it begins with the practice of kenosis.

And it seems that is what the dolphins and whales strive to inspire us to do by their example of unfailing kindness to us.

If we fail to awaken and respond, I wonder how we will bear the loneliness of living on this planet once the last dolphin has danced his finale across the horizon and the last whale has sung his final song? How will we manage without these sparkling entities in our midst to accompany us on the journey of life and anchor us in the hope that kindness, joy, and bliss can abide on this earth? Will we then wonder what we might have learned had we paused to notice that we are constantly in the presence of high beings just a few yards off our shores and to take a moment to tune in and listen to what it is they want us to know?

with tender patience, the dolphins hug our shores to dance for us, play with us, and win us over to love.

CHAPTER 17

the finale:
we too can do it

Dolphins can swim, jump, and spin higher and faster than is understandable for their size and configuration. Whales pull forty to fifty tons out of the water's depth to present themselves with amazing grace.

Both arrive out of nowhere in answer to a thought, a need for healing, or a prearranged encounter. They are filled with loving compassion, harmony, and grace, and speak through multiple channels at ultrasonic wavelengths. When we can't understand, they find a way to get through. They heal, they bring joy, and they evoke bliss. They are quite simply among the greatest beings in our midst.

During this journey with the dolphins, they have modeled the traits of the higher self for us and use their own prescription for manifesting a world of beauty. By focusing only on being their best, they create a powerful force field of clarity and joy and then bring it to our shores to share with us while using it to heal, teach, and pull us into it.

Their generous interactions with us not only stir and open our hearts but also stretch us to be more as they wait patiently for us to join them in the level they have attained. In their presence, we think of God and feel pulled into the force field of our highest potential.

When we accept these great beings as teachers and learn from them how to embody nothing but our ability to love all things at all times, the energy we generate from this invisible power will prove to be a force so strong it can twirl whales and spin galaxies. If we are willing to learn the lessons the dolphins have come to our shores to teach, we not only uncover the power of love but fulfill our purpose by pulling heaven through our hearts to our earth home and lives.

dolphins and whales
sing beneath the sea
and dance across the horizon,
beguiling us to join them in their
ballet of wisdom, love, harmony,
and joy—while waiting patiently
for us to arrive.

index

A Guidebook
4 - lightworkers

RIWE

Dg Wetman